T0113925

HELP TO GROW

THE BUILDING BLOCKS...WITH OVER 300
PREVAILING PRAYER POINTS, DECLARATIONS
AND 12 SCRIPTURAL NUGGETS.

DR. SUNDAY ODII

WESTBOW
P R E S S®
A DIVISION OF THOMAS NELSON
& ZONDERVAN

WestBow Press books may be ordered through
booksellers or by contacting:

WestBow Press
A Division of Thomas Nelson & Zondervan
1663 Liberty Drive
Bloomington, IN 47403
www.westbowpress.com
844-714-3454

ISBN: 978-1-6642-5331-5 (sc)
ISBN: 978-1-6642-5332-2 (e)

Print information available on the last page.

WestBow Press rev. date: 02/11/2022

DEDICATION

This book is dedicated to our Lord and Saviour Jesus Christ who remains the source of my strength., whose faithfulness I have benefited from far more than words can describe.

CONTENTS

FOREWORD

"Prof." as I called him due to his eclectic style of expression, is a genuine student of the Bible. His journey to Canada could be summarized as a faith adventure. Having attained some measure of success in his home country Nigeria, with attendant financial blessing, marital bliss and parenting of two lovely children, he left all to further his education in a strange land.

An experience in humility further endears him into my heart. I remember visiting him few days after joining our Church only to found out that his host family were Muslims. And through out his stay with this family nothing untoward was said about him.

Prof. went through myriads of challenges but came out with flying colours in his studies. Unlike most students, he had to work and study at the same time. He was favoured and loved by his employers as they noticed his dedication and diligence.

Sonnie had served in different capacities at the Church until the Holy Spirit got a perfect fit for him and he was appointed the Pastor of the teenage Church. We have since seen measurable transformation in the life of the teenagers. He was inspired to start a prayer meeting for the Children by the children, and this bi-monthly initiative is well received and loved by Children.

Help to grow, is an easy to read and implement, intelligent submission. I recommend you read this book as it will impact or transform your prayer and family life, and help solidify your relationship with God.

ACKNOWLEDGMENTS

_____

This book is a result of all the wisdom, knowledge, experiences, and opportunities afforded to me by God the Father whose love for me goes farther than my rebellion. I want to specifically acknowledge God the Son for his mercy, faithfulness, and unbounded largesse as well as the Holy Spirit who has helped in getting me to this point in my life.

I am eternally grateful to my mother and father for their care and support, and for preparing me as a child for life ahead.

*To my Zonal Pastor, Adeleke Aiku, thank you for praying for me at those dark times. Your prayers were helpful in pushing me through the finish line. Thank you for accepting to foreword this book. I'm so thankful.

*To Pastor (Mrs) Ebun Aiku, thank you for being my first audience to have had a sneak peak at what this book was all about. Thank for you for all your prayers and support. Thank you as well for those encouraging words at the time.

*To Gaylene Dempsey, thank you for the invaluable work you did, and ensuring that this book was written in simple language devoid of unnecessary vocabularies.

*To my two amazing children, Ella, and Uncle Sam, thank you so much for your love – along side laughter and cheekiness - which makes me chuckle every day and keeps me motivated so I can be a super good role model to you both.

*To my darling wife, you made my three years in Canada feel like time travels. Loving you comes naturally, and except Salvation, there's never been anything that can be compared to having a wife, mother, friend, partner, and sister combined in one amazing person. Thank you so much for holding the fort while I was away, I'm deeply grateful.

*To everyone who reads this book, thank you. I am truly honoured. I hope you will find the subtle and not so subtle side swipes in this book both magical and giggly.

PREFACE

I'm not an expert in praying and I do not intend to give such impression, but to my sublime thoughts there came the vision…it's been a long time coming. The global pandemic tipped open an outpouring for change resulting in borderless church and a spike in corporate prayers such that has never been recorded in modern history to the glory of God.

The Bible says:

Which none of the rulers of this age knew: for had they known it, they would not have crucified the Lord of glory (1 Corinthians 2:8 NKJV)

Even the COVID-19 virus serves His purpose. The lockdown and restrictions all serve God's purpose. Finally, the online church has come to stay.

My heart went pitter-patter as I heard the voice, "pen these things into a book" and from there it grew to something resembling a whooshing sound in my head. This came at the time I was overwhelmed emotionally having been away from my wife and children for an extended period.

Writing a Christian book has never really crossed my mind. I never thought I had anything to offer in this area. Besides, I was already busy devoting my spare time to writing a book on change management at the time, which I haven't finished, but I had to suspend it to start and finish this book.

At the start of this pandemic, I joined the prayer group of my local church in Canada, Hephzibah Parish of The Redeemed Christian Church of God and I must say that I have been greatly blessed by the teaching of my Zonal Pastor Adeleke Aiku whose love for prayer and God's Word has inspired me in my secret place. My growing interest in praying, especially finding time for a personal devotion coupled with an opportunity to pastor our teenage class, proved to be the icing on the cake. I am motivated to lead these teens into the early habit of finding God in the place of prayer and supporting them in praying their future through. That motivation culminated into the reason why this book was penned.

This book is divided into two parts. The first is centred around prayer, types of prayer and prayer points on various aspect of life. This book contains over 300 prevailing prayer points and prophetic declarations. The second part, entitled The Nuggets dwells on practical steps that can help Christians grow their walk with Jesus. These 12 Nuggets are a collection of Scriptural truths that can guide a child of God daily as we approach the end times.

This book started off as a prayer guide, but while I was writing, God laid on my heart to touch on various fundamental truths in God's Word that are crucial to sustaining our relationship with God. They are God's Word.

All Scripture is God-breathed and is useful for teaching, rebuking, correcting, and training in righteousness, so that the servant of God may be thoroughly equipped for every good work. (2 Timothy 3:16-17 NIV)

Let us talk a bit about the first part of the book, prayer. It is a conceded fact that the devotional character of Christians by no means keeps pace with their Christian faith. Prayer is the lubricant that keeps a child of God alive and active. Prayer is also the watchword and hallmark of true believers in their Kingdom pursuit and without it, worship becomes merely a lifeless apparatus.

This book reflects several deliberate efforts made since the onset of a pandemic toward spending time in God's Presence through heartfelt prayers. I have been a beneficiary of answered prayers through grace, mercy, and God's faithfulness. I have also had my share of unanswered prayers and I know what it is like to experience delay in answers to prayers.

The topics covered in this book are not a mere academic treatise. This book does not assert itself as a one-approach-fits-all to praying. Rather, it seeks to offer a profound and immeasurable approach to genuine prayer methodology. Reading a book does not automatically produce results, rather, outcomes are a consequence of the amount of energy you expend on putting it into practice. Just like repeatedly saying or quoting Jesus' teaching on prayer as contained in Luke 11:2-4, does not necessarily mean that your prayer will be answered.

While teaching teenagers, especially at the intercessory prayer group level, I observed the void that needs to be filled. Should this void be filled in good time, then we may have impacted the generation that precedes us. Regardless of age, if you truly love God, you will find this book helpful.

Over the course of time, I have become passionate about finding the answer to this question: why does the devil like them young and naïve? An article from the Harvard Centre on the Development titled Science of Early Childhood Development surmises

"All aspects of adult human capital, from workforce skills to cooperative and lawful behaviour, build on capacities that are developed during childhood, beginning at birth. When we invest wisely in our children and families, the next generation will pay that back through a lifetime of productivity and responsible citizenship."

This can only be accomplished through devotion and prayer. Therefore, this book is timely to be used for teenagers, youths, and new converts. I'm hoping that it will become an invaluable treasure to be cherished forever.

THE CATCH

I commend you for reading this book. If you bought this book yourself or someone else paid for it or you borrowed it to read and return, you're one of the few giants around. I promise that this small simple prayer book with Scriptural foundational nuggets on God's Word will bless your life. The effort you will pour in reading this book will be greatly rewarded.

The following words encouraged me greatly and shaped my perspective driving me from start to finish of this book.

"I would rather fail in a cause that will ultimately succeed than succeed in a cause that will ultimately fail." -Woodrow Wilson

The Bible also admonishes us:

And let us not get tired of doing what is good. At just the right time we will reap a harvest of blessings if we don't give up. (Galatians 6:9 NLT)

Writing this book is also a way of doing my bit and contributing to building my community. I want to point

Jesus as the Truth and the Way especially in a world where the wheel of moral decadence is spinning way too fast.

I can never express enough gratitude to my mom who tried her best to teach me this important principle. How I had wished I had taken it seriously at the time. My mom knows how to talk to the Lord in her native dialect. She wakes us up to pray in the morning and most of the time we'd go to sleep leaving her praying alone.

This book is a testament to God's supply of grace whenever it's needed by a believer. Grace for today!

I remember the story of Corrie ten Boom, who died in 1983. Corrie was a Dutch Christian who helped Jewish people escape the Nazis during the war and who was herself imprisoned at the age of 52. As a girl, Corrie asked her father Casper ten Boom whether she would be able to suffer without betraying her Lord Jesus Christ.

The story goes like this (I don't remember where and who had written it):

"Daddy, I am afraid that I will never be strong enough to be a martyr for Jesus Christ," said Corrie.

"Tell me, when you take a train from Haarlem to Amsterdam, when do I give you the money for the ticket? Three weeks before?" responded Casper.

"No, Daddy," said Corrie "You give me the money for the ticket just before we get on the train."

"That is right and so it is with God's strength," replied Casper. "Our wise Father in heaven knows when you are going to need things too. Today, you do not need the strength to be a martyr but as soon as you are called upon for the honour of facing death for Jesus, He will supply the strength you need just in time."

I believe this book is right for the time. God knew exactly when I needed the strength to pull all the stops and He supplied it – right in time. Grace! So, please put your nose in this book and I promise you it will be worth the read.

INTRODUCTION

For beginners, sometimes prayer can be scary and exhaustive. You set aside time to pray, and sleep comes encroaching into your prayer time. Then you find yourself struggling and squirming. Many of you recall what Jesus told his disciples,

Then he returned and found the disciples asleep. He said to Peter, "Simon, are you asleep? Couldn't you watch with me even one hour?" (Mark 14:37 NLT)

The disciples were literally tired and their eyes heavy with sleep, unaware of what was imminent at the time.

Let us begin by defining what a prayer is and what it is not. Prayer is a process of speaking, communing and communicating with God to build a relationship with Him. Prayer involves setting aside a time and if possible, a location to commune with God just as you would do with your friends or co-workers or parents or siblings.

For true believers, prayer is a dynamic interaction, not just a moment of silence. Prayer is as much a response to God as it is a request of God. Therefore, prayer is not just only a request of God, but a conversation with God. Prayer is a two-way conversation through which we grow in our relationship with God, so that we become more like Him. This involves talking and listening.

Prayer is not compelling God to do something He does not want to do. In other words, prayer is not manipulating God or trying to twist God's arm. Prayer is neither a monologue nor a therapeutic mantra of positive thinking, as it might be for Buddhists or even atheists. Prayer is not selfishly pleading or begging God and does not mean honouring ourselves in public.

And when you pray, do not be like the hypocrites, for they love to pray standing in the synagogues and on the street corners to be seen by others. Truly I tell you, they have received their reward in full. (Matthew 6:5 NIV)

The Pharisees feigned devoutness in public thereby receiving their reward from men and not from God. What they failed to understand is prayer is not so much a science that must be mastered by study or an art that is learned by public practice.

What are sermons, preaching and revivals without prayers? Just mere rhetorical orations or pulpit performance. Praying souls soon become prevailing saints and those who get farthest in prayer come to understand what God's will is on any issue than those who do not pray.

The efficacy and potency of the act of prayer may not be easily quantified.

Parents should endeavour to teach their children by example. Children tend to learn more by observation than by mere speaking – and the effectiveness of our prayer life should point our offspring to their own faith in God through fervent prayer.

It is spiritually toxic for parents to allow a child to suffer deprivation of the blessings of learning to know God and how to completely depend on Him because we are consumed in daily struggles. That is why the Lord admonishes parents to teach their children to pray and to walk uprightly before him.

Direct your children onto the right path, and when they are older, they will not leave it. (Proverbs 22:6 NLT)

"It is easier to build strong children than to repair broken men." -Frederick Douglass

"You can't teach an old dog new trick." John Fitzherbert's Book of Husbandry

Most people would agree that it's nearly impossible to change longstanding habits or ways, especially in an old person.

Recently, I learned some new stuff, but it was difficult. Learning at older age is hard unlike a child. It is an uphill climb to try to change someone at 40 years old. It takes extra self-discipline and courage to effect changes in adult than in children. So parents, I beseech you by the mercies of God, to do whatsoever you can to give your children the right foundation and correct building blocks that would sustain them on the journey ahead.

This is where prayer comes in handy. I believe that if we help our children to develop the habit of praying when they are still young, active and strong, then we are leaving behind a better generation and legacy of our lives.

Whether you are a child, teenager or an adult or even if you have recently accepted Jesus Christ as your Lord and Saviour or you have been a Christian your whole life, prayer is essential. Prayer sustains momentum and helps us to lead a victorious Christian life. Learning to pray God's Word will help you grow your faith.

Prayer is important and crucial to every believer who truly desires to maintain a right standing with God. Prayer is the linchpin of an effective relationship with God. Without fear of contradiction, I can say that prayer is neither for the heathen, agnostic or atheist nor for the good moral upstanding person.

Confess your sins to each other and pray for each other so that you may be healed. The earnest prayer of a righteous person has great power and produces wonderful results. (James 5:16 NLT)

Pray without ceasing. (1 Thessalonians 5:17 KJV)

And pray in the spirit on all occasions with all kinds of prayers and requests. With this in mind, be alert and always keep on praying for all the Lord's people. (Ephesians 6:18 NIV)

King David prayed his way through victories and successes his entire life and the Bible tells us that Daniel prayed every day. Regardless of what the situation is, believers need to pray always. If we want to know and do the Father's will, we must pray constantly and in the Spirit. Jesus could not do the Father's work without praying and receiving revelation from Him.

So, Jesus explained,

I tell you the truth, the Son can do nothing by himself. He does only what he sees the Father doing. Whatever the Father does, the Son also does. (John 5:19 NLT).

Prayer is the cornerstone of the life of every believer or true Christian.

Apostle Paul says,

Devote yourself to prayer, being watchful and thankful. (Colossians 4:2 NIV)

Prevailing Prayer provides every believer with a place to encounter God's supernatural presence and His life-changing Word. Jesus Christ, our Saviour as the eternal Word of God gives us an insight into the appropriate way to give thanks and make requests in prayers.

THE LORD'S PRAYER

...A STRUCTURED MODEL

In Luke 11:1, the disciples asked Jesus to teach them how to pray. Consequently, Jesus Christ taught them in a simple manner and modelled what can be described as a prayer template. The prayer is often known as our Lord's prayer:

Pray like this: Our Father in heaven, may your name be kept holy. May your Kingdom come soon. May your will be done on earth, as it is in heaven. Give us today the food we need, and forgive us our sins, as we have forgiven those who sin against us. And don't let us yield to temptation but rescue us from the evil one. (Matthew 6:9-13 NLT)

Let's look at it in King James Version as well.

After this manner therefore pray ye: Our Father which art in heaven, Hallowed be thy name.

Thy kingdom come, Thy will be done in earth, as it is in heaven.

Give us this day our daily bread.

And forgive us our debts, as we forgive our debtors.

And lead us not into temptation but deliver us from evil: For thine is the kingdom, and the power, and the glory, for ever. Amen. (Matthew 6:9-13 KJV).

Our Lord's prayer in Matthew 6:9-13, which is often referred to as Sermon on the Mount, is a prayer that provides us with an archetype. It is simply a model prayer and does not always have to be repeated. More than any other prayer, it has shaped believers throughout the ages. All encompassing, it influences the minutest details and nitty-gritty of our daily lives as Christians.

God has used this simple, but profound prayer to teach us some lessons in most precious ways. In fact, God has taught me personal fundamental strategies for putting to death the uprisings of sin – especially the subtle ones – in my heart.

Our Lord's Prayer has five main components:

1. *Hallowed be thy name* – Right off the bat you will observe that this prayer does not start with a petition or request. Why? We know the great multitudes surrounding God's throne are not making petitions but giving thanks and worshipping God our creator. Our Lord's prayer begins with adoration.

2. *Thy Kingdom come, thy will be done* – After worship comes consecration, which is setting yourself apart in spirit, soul and body for God's exclusive use. As a believer, pray that God will move His kingdom forward through you. In Gethsemane, we saw how Jesus surrendered his entire life to God's exclusive use:

   Father, if you are willing, please take this cup of suffering away from me. Yet I want your will to be done, not mine. (Luke 22:42 NLT)

   Jesus surrendered His everything to God's will. The secret to all of God is all of you. This is an act of consecration and complete surrender!

3. *Give us our daily bread* – Now, going by the model provided by our Lord and Saviour Jesus Christ, you can introduce your requests. Worship God first, consecrate yourself and surrender completely to His will, then make your requests known unto Him. Whatever you need, go ahead and ask Him. Sometimes as Christians, we get our wants mixed up with our needs. We must be specific and ask according to His will. It would be logical and great that we could be happy people if we had all our basic needs met, but so often we are not. Even with our needs met, we stress out anxiously over our wants. Take a moment right now and painstakingly go through the items on the list of what you are asking God to see if they are reasonable and logical. Above all, are they in line with God's will for you? Then share your answers with God sincerely in

your next prayer. Make your supplication known before God.

4. *And forgive us our debts as we forgive our debtors –* This is more of an intercessory prayer. Intercession is when you stand in the gap between an offended God and an offensive person or situation. The secret of coming out of bitterness or madness at someone is to pray and intercede, asking God to be merciful to such a person or situation. It's highly improbable to remain bitter when you are asking God to show mercy. Jesus is the great intercessor. Jesus in his priestly prayer (John 17:1-26), prayed the whole 26 verses glorifying God and asking God to preserve the disciples prior to His ascension. Daniel prayed 15 verses interceding for the children of Israelites asking God to forgive them (Daniel 9). This is what real intercession looks like.

5. *And lead us not into temptation but deliver us from evil–* Satan is real and temptations are his work. We have an enemy whose primary agenda is to destroy God's people. Every day believers must put on the whole armour of God to be able to resist every evil attack from the enemy (Ephesians 6). The Bible makes it clear that there is a devil. Satan is a created being, an angel who rebelled against God and took a third of the angels with him and is now bent on destroying the people of God. He is called by many names: the adversary, working against the people of God; the accuser of the brethren, accusing us before God; the ruler of this world as well as the tempter, testing us to leave or disobey God. He is

a roaring lion seeking who he can devour and he disguises himself as an angel of light. He is the thief who comes to steal, kill and destroy. Therefore, we are encouraged to put on the whole armour of God to withstand the attacks from the accuser of the brethren.

I know that some people would argue that this component of the prayer of protection is like making a request and hence, more of a repetition. However, the interesting thing about this petition is that grammatically it is in the form of parallelism. What does that mean? It means a statement is made, then repeated and developed. This first part says, *lead us not into temptation.* The second part develops it and adds to it by saying, *"deliver us from evil.* There isn't just temptation; there is also the evil one to reckon with. In addition, we have an example of litotes, which is a form of figure of speech which negates a positive to convey understated irony. In order words, you're stating something both positively and negatively to emphasize a point.

Our Lord's prayer is like a diamond that can reflect fresh light enhancing its beauty as we examine it more closely. This passage of the Scripture not only teaches us about prayer, but also about Christian living. It is one of those scriptural passages in the New Testament that makes it crystal clear that praying and living are two sides of the same coin.

PRAYER OF SALVATION

Because if you confess with your mouth that Jesus is Lord and believe in your heart that God raised him from the dead, you will be saved. For with the heart, one believes and is justified, and with the mouth one confesses and is saved. (Romans 10:9-10 ESV)

Typically, this is a prayer that is said when someone repents of their sins and wants to give their life to Jesus Christ. This sort of prayer is called the salvation prayer and it's also known as the sinner's prayer.

Prayer of Salvation is the most important prayer. When you are ready to begin your eternal journey with your maker, when you are ready to become a true Christian in the real sense of the word, only then would you say the prayer of salvation. God is waiting and has given us assurance in His Word to answer us whenever we call on Him.

Everyone who calls on the name of the Lord will be saved. (Romans 10:13 NIV)

Before you begin your new journey with Christ, it is important to establish a right relationship with your maker, Jesus Christ through the simple ABC of salvation.

A - Accepting
B - Believing
C - Confessing

For God so loved the world that he gave his one and only Son, that whoever believes in him, shall not perish but have eternal life. (John 3:16 NIV)

God loves you, and He has got a plan for you.

While the thief (devil) comes only but to kill, steal and destroy, Jesus came to give us life. In the word of Jesus, He says,

I came that they may have life and have it abundantly. (John 10:10 ESV)

When God created the first man and woman, Adam and Eve, and left them in a beautiful garden of Eden, they became sinful through disobedience and sin entered the world. The Bible says,

For all have sinned and fall short of the glory of God. (Romans 3:23 NIV)

This resulted in death, a separation from God and consequently ruined the once amazing relationship that man had with God.

God in His abundant mercy out of love, sent His only begotten son to die for you and your sins. Jesus died for our sins, He was buried and raised from the grave on the third day (1 Corinthians 15:3-4). This singular act brought salvation to the world and reconciled man to God again. Jesus paid for the sins of the world, accomplishing the single most important event in the history, far greater than anything the world had ever seen or known.

If you really want to appreciate what Jesus did on that cross, then you must accept Jesus as the only way to God. Jesus said,

I am the way, and the truth, and the life, no one comes to the father, except through me (John 14:6 ESV)

We are saved by God's grace and salvation can not be earned. All you need to do is simple:

Accept you are a sinner
Believe that Jesus Christ died for your sins
Confess your sins by asking His forgiveness.
This is true repentance.

From the depth of your heart, you can say this simple repentance-salvation prayer:

My Father and my God, today I accept that I am a sinner and that I have sinned against you. I believe that Jesus Christ your Son came to this world and died for my sin, and You raised Him from dead to life. I therefore confess Him as my Lord and personal Saviour, and from this day forward, I surrender the whole of my life and being to Him. Father, Lead me, help me, and guide me to do your will forever and never to return to my old ways. This I pray in Jesus' name. Amen.

If you have sincerely and honestly prayed the above prayer from the depth of your heart, congratulations!

Having prayed the above prayer, join any church that is deeply rooted with the Word of God so you can begin to enjoy the endless peace that comes from the joy of salvation, the unbounded largesse of assurance of answering your prayers. Begin to do exploits for God as you engage in winning souls for Christ as well.

ASSURANCE OF ANSWERED PRAYERS

Prayer becomes a lifeless exercise in futility when you are not expecting answers, but fortunately God has given man assurance of answered prayers. Jesus says,

"Ask, and it will be given to you; seek, and you will find; knock, and it will be opened to you. For everyone who asks, receives, and he who seeks finds, and to him who knocks it will be opened." (Matthew 7:7-8 NKJV)

"You haven't done this before. Ask, using my name, and you will receive, and you will have abundant joy." (John 16:24 NLT)

I see prayer as a privilege of touching the heart of the Father through Jesus and it is an exercise of faith and hope. God wants us to come boldly to the throne of grace and into his presence so we may obtain mercy and find grace to help in times of need (Hebrews 4:16) and He wants us to ask Him anything (Philippians 4:6). We are fortunate to have God's full and everlasting love, He loves us so much that He's interested in us and our needs.

However, to assume that a prayer is unanswered because you do not receive what you asked for is to misunderstand both God and prayer. In the words of Jesus:

Do not be like them, for your Father knows what you need before you ask him (Matthew 6:8 NIV)

This is the confidence which we have in approaching God, that if we ask anything according to His will, He hears us. And if we know that he hears us, whatever we ask – we know that we have what we asked of Him. (1 John 5:14-15 NIV)

Jesus also tells us in the gospel of John,

If you abide in Me, and My Words abide in you, ask whatever you wish, and it will be done for you. (John 15:17 ESV)

Always check the motive behind your request or petition.

When you ask, you do not receive, because you ask with wrong motives, that you may spend what you get on your pleasures. (James 4:3 NIV)

Why are you making that petition? Is the motive behind that request for a car right or is it to make a splash? Why do you want to purchase that dress? Is it because you want to dress to impress? Ask yourself if your appeal is in line with the will of God. I know that sometimes accepting God's will in times of trial can be like a test. Personally, I have been there and I can relate.

Apostle Paul says in his letter to the Corinthians:

All things are lawful for me, but not all things are helpful; all things are lawful for me, but not all things edify. (1 Corinthians 10:23 NKJV)

One aspect of praying amiss is praying for things that are not expedient for us.

Pray points:

Father, please help me identify those things that I really need and are Your will, so I don't ask amiss in the mighty name of Jesus.

Father, help me to ask according to thy will, O Lord.

PRAYING
THE SCRIPTURE

———————

I am a latecomer to praying the Scripture as I started not too long ago. It's one of my regrets and I wish I could turn back time to correct my mistake. I urge you to start praying Scripture early in life. My mom does this fantastically in her native language and it is almost like she is speaking in tongues. Nonetheless, praying the Scripture has broadened and deepened my prayer life.

Here are a few prayer types and points from the Scripture.

Our Lord Jesus Christ modelled what a typical prayer should look like to us in Matthew 6:5-13 and that prayer begins in thanksgiving. In this book, we offer a few types of prayer and their examples.

Prayer of Praise and Thanksgiving

When you study the letters written by Apostle Paul in the Scripture, you will observe how he was always giving thanks to God and he always begins his letters with thanksgiving.

- *Be careful for nothing, but in every thing by prayer and supplication with thanksgiving let your requests be made known unto God. (Philippians 4:6 KJB)*
- *I have not stopped giving thanks for you remembering you in my prayers (Ephesians 1:16 NIV)*
- *First, I thank my God through Jesus Christ for you all, that your faith is spoken of throughout the whole world. (Romans 1:8 NKJV)*
- *I always thank God for you because of his grace given you in Christ Jesus. (1 Corinthians 1:4 NIV)*

David, on the other hand, offered praise to God. Praise is the declaration of the truth about who God is, what He has done and what He promises to do. (Psalm 150:6)

- *O Lord, our God, how majestic is your name in all the earth! You have set your glory above the heavens. (Psalm 8:1 ESV)*
- *Bless the Lord, O my soul, and all that is within me, bless his holy name! (Psalm 103:1 ESV)*

Prayer of Agreement – two or more persons praying and agreeing on earth unto heaven about a matter or a particular situation (Matthew 18;19-20; Acts 1:14; Acts 4:24)

Prayer of Confession – Acknowledging your sin before God, and declaring or confessing them out (James 5:16; 1 John 1:9; Leviticus 5:5; Psalm 32:5)

Prayer of Fellowship – Spending time with God in an activity prayerfully (Psalm 55:14; 1 John 1:7; Acts 2:42)

Prayer of Intercession – Praying for the needs of other persons, situations, or nations (2 Corinthians 1:11; Psalm 122:6; Philippians 1:9)

Prayer of Petition – A petition is basically making a request, identifying a need and praying for it. When we pray, we're asking God to fulfill our needs (Philippians 4:6-7; 1 John 5;15; Philippians 4:19)

Prayer of Praise – In a prayer of praise or worship, we exalt the greatness of God and acknowledge our dependence on Him in all things (Hebrews 13:15-16; Psalm 7:17b; Psalm 69:30; 1 Samuel 2:1-10)

Prophetic Prayer – Receiving a word or message from God for someone else or a nation. This is a prayer in specific circumstances. It is often described as the act of commanding God's prophetic vision to be fulfilled on earth thereby accomplishing God's will (Amos 3:7; Proverbs 25:2; Daniel 2:22)

Prayer of Salvation – This is a prayer that is said when a sinner confesses and repents of their sin, turns from their evil ways, and asks God for forgiveness and states their belief in Jesus' life, death and his saving resurrection (Romans 10:9-10; Psalm 51; John 3:16)

Prayer of Thanksgiving – Showing appreciation by offering thanks to God (Psalm 9:1; Psalm 7:17a; Psalm 35:18)

Praying in Tongues – Praying in a personal spiritual language that edifies you in your relationship with God (1 Corinthians 14:13-14; 14:2,4; 18:9-10; Romans 8:26; Acts 10:44-46)

Praying by listening – While the Bible does not categorically mention listening as a prayer, the concept of prayer by listening is based on prayer as a two-way communication. We talk, we listen and God responds. Sitting at the feet of the Master and listening to Him is one way we can hear his small still voice (1 Kings 19:12-13; John 10:27)

Prayer of warfare – Pushing back against Satan and his demons with the weapons of God's kingdom (Isaiah 54:17; 1 Peter 5:8-9; James 4:7; Ephesians 6:12)

PRAYER OF THANKSGIVING

The Scripture encourages us to always give thanks to God. Thanksgiving prayers are an important part of the believer's life. It is a spiritual discipline necessary for daily living.

Oh, give thanks to the Lord, for He is good, for his steadfast love endures forever. (Psalm 107:1 ESV)

I will give thanks to the Lord because of his righteousness, I will sing the praise to the name of the Lord Most High. (Psalm 7:17 NIV)

The more you profess gratitude, the more you will observe things to be grateful for. Simply put, the human heart responds readily to exercise. Take a moment every day to ruminate on and appreciate God's love around you and write down what you perceive.

The refrain in the beautiful hymn written by Johnson Oatman, Jr says:

Count your blessings, name them one by one,
Count your blessings, see what God has done!
Count your blessings, name them one by one,
And it will surprise you what the Lord has done.

Perhaps you should get a piece of paper and write down what God has done in your life. Write both the big and seemingly small things. You will be amazed at how many things the Lord has done for you and surprised to see how gratitude can alter your viewpoint and give you even more reasons to praise and worship God.

PRAYER POINTS:

1. Lord, I give You thanks because You are good. (1 Chronicles 16:34)
2. Lord, I give You thanks because You are righteous, and I will sing the praises of Your name. (Psalm 7:17)
3. I thank You Lord with all my heart. (Psalm 9:1)
4. Father, I will give You thanks and glorify You in songs. (Psalm 69:30)
5. I praise You Lord because You are a great king above all gods. (Psalm 95:3)
6. Father, I praise You because You are good, and Your mercy endures forever. (Psalm 106:1)
7. Lord, I devote myself to prayer, to be watchful and thankful. (Colossians 4:2)
8. Thank You, Lord, because You are a consuming fire. (Hebrews 12:28)

9. Thank You, Lord, for being the rock of my salvation. (Psalm 95:1-5)

10. Father, I thank You because this is the day that You have made, and I will rejoice and be glad in it. (Psalm 118:24)

11. Father, I thank You because You have been glorious to me and my family. (1 Chronicles 29:13)

12. Father, I thank You because You have redeemed me and for Your steadfast love. (Psalm 107:1-3)

13. Thank You, Father, because You are upright and just. (Psalm 119:1-8)

14. Father, I thank You so much for Your grace upon my life and everything that concerns me. (1 Corinthians 1:4)

15. Father, I thank You for everything. Thank You because You're beautiful and You're beautiful for every circumstance. (1 Thessalonians 5:16-18)

16. Dear Lord, I thank You for being my strength, my shield and my helper. (Psalm 28:7)

17. Father, I thank You and praise Your glorious name. (1 Chronicles 29:13)

18. Father, thank You for Your unfailing love and wonderful deeds. (Psalm 107:8)

19. Father, thank You for satisfying my mouth with good things. (Psalm 107:9)

20. Father, thank You for Your provisions and supernatural supplies. (2 Corinthians 9:10)

21. Thank You for daily loading me with Your benefits. (Psalm 68:19)

22. Lord, thank You for enlarging my harvest and increasing my joy. (Isaiah 9:3)

23. Father, I praise You for blessing the works of my hands. (Psalm 67:6)

24. Father, thank You for Your outstretched hands of love and for not abandoning me. (Hebrews 13:5b)

25. Father, I thank You sincerely from the depth of my heart for all Your wonderful acts over my life. (Psalm 9:1)

26. Father, thank You for Your blessings that make me rich in spirit, soul and body. (2 Corinthians 9:11)

27. Father, I magnify Your name because Your name is great. (Psalm 69:30)

28. Dear Lord, thank You for blossoming my life like flowers and rooting it like cedars of Lebanon. (Hosea 14:5-6)

29. Father, thank You for making my life as beautiful as the forest of Lebanon (Psalm 72:16)

30. Father, thank You preparing and calling me out of obscure beginning to a glorious destiny. (2 Timothy 1:9)

PRAYER OF FORGIVENESS AND MERCY

To repent is more than simply asking God's forgiveness. It entails a deliberate effort to lead a life devoid of sin. The prayer of forgiveness is important when seeking restoration and reconciliation with God.

From a spiritual standpoint, we were all born into sin.

For all have sinned and fall short of the glory of God. (Romans 3:23 NKJV)

Without God's pardon, we would be lost forever and eternally separated form our maker. In Romans 6:23, we are warned the consequence of sin is death, a spiritual separation from God.

The Scripture tells us that our God is full of mercy

Have mercy on me, O God, according to your unfailing love, according to your great compassion blot out my transgressions. Wash away all my iniquity and cleanse me from my sin. For I know my transgressions, and my sin is always before me. (Psalm 51:1-3 NIV)

It is equally important to forgive others. Jesus died for our sins and if we want Him to forgive us, then we must be willing and ready to forgive those who have offended us.

"When you forgive others, you in no way change the past, but you sure do change the future." –Bernard Meltzer, Radio Host

Mercy, on the other hand, is one of the attributes of God. The prayer of mercy is for every child of God to pray given our imperfections. It is only through God's mercy that we can overcome and remain faithful. His mercy and forgiveness are essential in our walk with Christ because the flesh will always fail us.

"The best of man is still man" – Pastor Adeleke Aiku

We are completely dependent on God for everything starting from oxygen to our most basic needs, and without God's mercy, the enemy would make mincemeat of us.

For he says to Moses, "I will have mercy on whom I will have mercy and I will have compassion on whom I will have compassion." (Romans 9:15-16 NIV)

PRAYER POINTS:

1. Father, thank You for another opportunity to come before you this day to ask for Your forgiveness.

2. Father, I have sinned against You and I am not worthy to be called your child. Be merciful unto me, a sinner today in the mighty name of Jesus. (Luke 15:18; Luke 18:13)

3. Father, please forgive me for all my sins, both intentional and unintentional, in the mighty name of Jesus. (Leviticus 4:2 ESV; Numbers 15:22 ESV)

4. Father, I am sorry for all my sins. I come to You with a heavy heart, please help me. (Isaiah 41:10)

5. Father, I know You detest my sin and it is an abomination to you. Lord, please forgive me. (1 Peter 3:12; Proverbs 28:9)

6. O satisfy us early with Your mercy, that we may rejoice and be glad all our days. (Psalm 90:14)

7. Thank you, Lord, for Your mercy endures forever. (1 Chronicles 16:34)

8. Thank you, Lord, because You are a God of great mercy. (Psalm 103:8)

9. Have mercy upon me, O God. (Psalm 86:3-6)

10. Oh Lord, pardon my sins by the greatness of Your mercy. (Numbers 14:19)

11. Father, cause me to enjoy and share in the abundance of Your mercy. (Ephesians 2:4)

12. O Lord, grant me Your mercy that is great above the heavens. (Psalm 108:4)

13. Father, have mercy upon me and deliver me from all my troubles. (Psalm 25:17)

14. Oh Lord, by Your mercy, deliver me from death. (Psalm 116:8)

15. Almighty God, have mercy upon my dwelling place. (Jeremiah 30:8)

16. Father, by Your mercy, do not let anyone swallow me. (Psalm 56:1)

17. Father, let Your mercy exalt my horn among my peers, colleagues, and friends. (Psalm 89:24)

18. O Lord, by Your mercy, I am free from every evil consumption. (Lamentations 3:22-23)

19. Father, according to Your Word, let only Your goodness and mercy be my daily companion in the mighty name of Jesus. (Psalm 23:6)

20. Father, by Your mercy, deliver me from distress and pains. Oh God of my salvation, give me relief from disaster and distress in the mighty name of Jesus. (Psalm 4:1)

21. O Lord, show me Your mercy and grant me thy salvation in the mighty name of Jesus. (Psalm 85:7)

22. Father, I come to You Lord, in the multitude and abundance of Your mercy. (Psalm 5:7)

23. O Lord, in your multitude of mercy, hear my prayer and accept my worship in the mighty name of Jesus. (Psalm 5:1-7)

24. Father, have compassion on me and cast my sins into the depth of the sea. (Micah 7:19)

25. My Father and my God, have mercy upon me and cleanse me by the blood of Christ from the stains and guilt of my sins. (1 John 1:7)

26. Father, wash me thoroughly from all guilt and condemnation, and I shall be clean in the mighty name of Jesus. (Psalm 51:1)

PRAYER FOR DELIVERANCE AND HEALING

The Bible tells us:

If My people who are called by name will humble themselves, and pray and seek My face, and turn from their wicked ways then I will hear from heaven, and I will forgive their sin and will heal their land. (2 Chronicles 7:14 NKJV)

And the prayer of faith shall save the sick, and the Lord shall raise him up; and if he has committed sins, they shall be forgiven him. (James 5:15 KJV)

And suddenly, a woman who had a flow of blood for twelve years came from behind and touched the hem of His garment. For she said to herself, "If only I may touch His garment, I shall be made well." But Jesus turned around, and when He saw her, He said, "Be of good cheer, daughter; your faith has made

you well." And the woman was made well from that hour.
(Matthew 9:20-22 NKJV)

Here are some prayer points for healing and deliverance that you can pray scripturally.

1. Father, thank you for all the healings and deliverances that I have been enjoying over time. (Psalm 103:1-4)
2. Father Lord, protect me from trouble and surround me with the songs of deliverance. (Psalm 32:7)
3. Father, by your stripes I am healed in Jesus' name. (1 Peter 2:24)
4. Father, heal me and repair every damage cell, tissues, organ or system in my body. (Jeremiah 17:14)
5. Lord cause my health to spring forth and make me whole. (Jeremiah 33:36)
6. Dear Lord, by the authority in the name of Jesus, uproot every form of malady in my body and let sickness lose its hold in my life in Jesus' name. (Matthew 10:1)
7. Lord, strengthen me and send help to me from Zion. Take away every form of sickness and disease from my life in the mighty name of Jesus. (Isaiah 41:10)
8. Father take away from my body every sickness and let my body be free from every disease in the mighty name of Jesus. (Deuteronomy 7:15)
9. Father, let me be in sound health and cause me to prosper. Father, I know you have power to bring healing into both my body, my heart and spirit. (3 John 1:2)

10. Father, in line with your promises, restore my soul and well being in the mighty name of Jesus. (Psalm 23:3)

11. Lord, in line with your death, resurrection and assurance of your ascension, I surrender to you my medical report, my health and doctor's prognosis and lay them before your throne in the mighty name of Jesus. (Hebrews 4:16)

12. Father, like the woman who was too shy to come to you, but instead resorted to grabbing the hem of your garment, please make me whole today in the name of Jesus. (Matthew 9:20-22)

13. Father, heal my children and all my offspring in the mighty name of Jesus. (Matthew 15:22-27)

14. I decree, that the Lord has forgiven me and has healed all my diseases in Jesus' name. (Psalm 103:3)

15. Every dead tissue or organ in my body, receive life now in the name of Jesus. (Isaiah 53:1-5)

16. I curse and rebuke every spirit of ulcer, headaches, abdominal pains, and cancer that attempt to establish itself in any part of my body in the name of Jesus. (Genesis 27:29)

17. I lose myself from a weakened immune system and I curse its root to die from today in the mighty name of Jesus. (Psalm 107:19-21)

18. Father, I believe whosoever shall call on your name shall be saved. Daddy, I call upon you today for my deliverance in the mighty name of Jesus. (Acts 2:21)

19. Father, destroy the work of the devil in my life and deliver me from any form of sickness in the mighty name of Jesus. (1 John 3:8)

20. Daddy, please visit every part of my body today and as a skillful surgeon, come and perform surgery

that doctors of this world cannot understand in the mighty name of Jesus. (Deuteronomy 7:15)

21. Father, deliver me from every form of affliction in the mighty name of Jesus. (Psalm 34:19)

PRAYER FOR GOD'S PROTECTION

―――――――

It's an instinct to seek to protect the stuffs we cherish most in our lives and unfortunately, there are practically no safe places anymore. Even in our personal homes, evil and danger seem to intrude on our lives with devastating swiftness. The upside is that our loving God has assured us of His protection whenever we need it and ask for it. Regardless of the danger you are in or the scary situation facing you, never underestimate what the power of prayer can do.

The Scripture tells of God's protection in Psalm 121:

I will lift up mine eyes unto the hills, from whence cometh my help. My help cometh from the Lord, which made heaven and earth. He will not suffer thy foot to be moved: he that keepeth thee will not slumber. Behold, he that keepeth Israel shall neither slumber nor sleep. The Lord is thy keeper: the Lord is thy shade upon thy right hand. The sun shall not smite thee by day, nor the moon by the night. The Lord shall preserve thee from all evil: he shall preserve thy soul. The Lord shall preserve thy going out and thy coming in from this time forth, and even forever more. (Psalm 121 KJV)

PRAYER POINTS:

1. Father Lord, I thank and praise you for being my rock and shield and I am grateful that I can go to sleep and count on your protection any day any time. (Psalm 28:7)
2. Father, deliver me from every evil work and preserve me for thy name's sake. (2 Timothy 4:18)
3. Father, deliver me and my household from the snare of the fowler and perilous pestilence. (Psalm 91:3)
4. Father, no weapon fashioned against me shall prosper in the mighty name of Jesus. (Isaiah 54:17)
5. Father, condemn any tongue that shall rise against me and my household in judgment in the mighty name of Jesus. (Isaiah 54:17)
6. O Lord, I take refuge in you and from today shield me with your favour in the mighty name of Jesus. (Psalm 5:11-12)
7. Father, spread your protection over me and my family so that we will rejoice in you, our God of salvation in the mighty name of Jesus. (Habakkuk 3:18).
8. Father, as I dwell in your secret place, please hide me and my household under your shadow in the mighty name of Jesus. (Psalm 91:1)
9. Father do not allow the fire of life to burn me and my family in Jesus' name. (Isaiah 43:2)
10. My father and my God, preserve my comings and goings all the days of my life in the mighty name of Jesus. (Isaiah 43:2).

11. Father, do not let me be carried away by the flood or storm of life. (Matthew 8:24-27)

12. Father, protect me for I am the apple of your eye. (Psalm 17:8)

13. Everlasting Father, keep me protected from every fiery furnace of the enemy in the mighty name of Jesus. (Daniel 3:23-26)

14. Father, by your wisdom, protect and preserve me from the way of the evil man in the mighty name of Jesus. (Psalm 140:1)

15. Father, hear me in the day of trouble and may the God of Jacob defend me. (Psalm 20:1-2)

16. Father, in the name of Jesus, I receive strength from Zion in Jesus' name. (Psalm 20:2)

17. Father, build a wall of fire around me and my family in the mighty name of Jesus. (Zachariah 2:5)

18. Father, uphold me and my family, with thy right hand of righteousness and strengthen me in the mighty name of Jesus. (1saiah 41:10)

19. Father, according to thy promises, do not fail or forsake me in the day of trouble in Jesus' name. (Deuteronomy 31:6)

20. Father, according to thy promises, protect me and my household from those who malign us and keep us safe from the hands of the wicked in the mighty name of Jesus. (Psalm 12:5-7)

21. Father, the mindset on the flesh is death, but the mindset on the Spirit is life and peace. Lord, I ask that you protect my mind from every mindset on the flesh in Jesus' name. (Romans 8:6)

This sweet hymn does remind me that protection can only come from Jesus Christ

Christ be with me, Christ within me,
Christ behind me, Christ before me,
Christ beside me, Christ to win me,
Christ to comfort and restore me.
Christ beneath me, Christ above me,
Christ in quiet, Christ in danger,
Christ in hearts of all that love me,
Christ in mouth of friend and stranger.
-St Patrick's Breastplate

Let everything be centred on Christ Jesus because all other ground is sinking sand

PRAYER
FOR ABUNDANCE

For I know the plans I have for you, declares the Lord, plans to prosper you and not to harm you. Plans to give you hope and a future. (Jeremiah 29:11 NIV)

God does not want us to eke out existence, so He sent His only begotten son, Jesus to come to this sinful world to give us life. Not only that, He also came to give us a life that is full and rich, and satisfying. Jesus says:

The thief does not come except to steal and to kill and to destroy. I have come that they may have life, and that they my have it more abundantly. (John 10:10 NKJV)

And Jabez called on the God of Israel saying, "Oh, that You would bless me indeed, and enlarge my territory, that Your hand would be with me, and that You would keep me from evil, that I may not cause pain." So God granted him what he requested. (1 Chronicles 4:10 NKJV)

Are you looking for an abundant life and something to fill you? If yes, then pray to God to bless you abundantly.

PRAYER POINTS:

1. I lift my voice and praise Your name Lord for Your wonderful provisions in Your life. (Psalm 59:17)
2. Father, supply every of my need according to Your riches in Christ Jesus in the mighty name of Jesus. (Philippians 4:19)
3. From today, Lord let me enjoy abundance in Your love, mercy and glory in Jesus' name. (Psalm 5:7)
4. Father, let my cup run over and overflow as You prepare a table before me in the presence of my enemies in Jesus' name. (Psalm 23:5)
5. Father, bless me abundantly and let Your gifts fill my cup until it overflows. (Psalm 23:5)
6. Father, please let my cup run over to all my generations in Jesus' name. (Psalm 23)
7. Father, bless me with the riches of faith and the prosperity of faith, mercy and grace, so that my treasure will be stored up in heaven in the mighty name of Jesus. (Matthew 6:19-20)
8. Lord, You made the ravens feed Elijah. Let it happen to my life in Jesus' name. (1 Kings 17:2-6)
9. Father, provide for me and my family abundantly in the mighty name of Jesus. (John 6:1-12)
10. I delight myself in the word of the Lord therefore, I am blessed. Wealth and riches shall be in my house in Jesus' name. (Psalm 112:1-3)
11. In the name of Jesus of Nazareth, with me are riches and honour, enduring wealth and prosperity in the mighty name of Jesus. (Proverbs 8:18)

12. The Lord is my shepherd, and I shall not want. (Psalm 23:1)

13. Father, in the name of Jesus, I receive wealth from You and the good health to enjoy it. (Ecclesiastes 5:19)

14. Father, give me and my household abundant life in the mighty name of Jesus. (John 10:10)

15. Father, in the name of Jesus, Abraham's blessings are mine. Lord, please give me an Abrahamic abundance blessing in the mighty name of Jesus. (Galatians 3:14)

16. I am prospering in every way. My body keeps well, even as my soul keeps well and prospers. (3 John 2)

17. Father, as I have given, it shall be given in return to me. Good measure, pressed down, shaken together, running over, shall men give into my life. For with the same measure that I give, it shall be given to me. (Luke 6:38)

18. Father, I am blessed and shall not suffer any lack because I trust in You. Although, the Young lions do lack and suffer hunger, but I shall not want any good thing (Psalm 34:8-10)

19. Father, annihilate poverty in my generation in the mighty name of Jesus. (2 Corinthians 8:9)

20. I seek first the kingdom of God, therefore everything that I need shall be added unto me. (Matthew 6:33)

21. I am like a tree that is planted by the riverside of the water. Everything I do shall prosper. (Psalm 1:3)

22. My God shall supply all my needs according to His riches in glory by Christ Jesus. (Philippians 4:19)

PRAYER FOR DIVINE FAVOUR

Favour is when God gives us what we do not deserve. In the Bible, God chose Gideon, not because he deserved it or that he was the best choice, but divine favour picked him and made him the judge of Israel (Judges 6:11-23). We serve a God of unconditional favour, there is nothing we do to deserve it, but God chose us in Christ, We did not do anything to deserve it, He chose us, loved us and blessed us, hallelujah.

David is a good case to study. If you dig into 1 Samuel 16:1-13 and 2 Samuel 6:21, you will see that David was made king by the divine favour of God. He neither deserved it, nor was he the best choice.

And Joseph found grace in his sight, and he served him; and he made him overseer over the house, and all that he had put into his hand. (Genesis 39:4 KJV)

Joseph was 17 when his brothers sold him. It took him 13 years of hardship and earthly misery to receive what God had in store for him. However, from the Scripture we learn that everywhere Joseph went, he was indeed blessed. Every time Satan attempted to destroy him and torpedo his destiny, God gave him favour.

God is still in the business of bestowing and honouring His children with even bigger favour than the kind Joseph received. Jesus is the same yesterday, today and forever.

PRAYER POINTS:

1. Father, I thank You that Your favour surrounds me like a shield. (Psalm 5:12)
2. Father, I thank You that I have found favour in Your sight. (Ruth 2:13)
3. Our God and our King, I thank You for all Your divine favour that I have enjoyed over time. (2 Samuel 2:6; Psalm 90:17)
4. Father, thank You for encompassing me with endless favour in Jesus' name (Proverbs 18:22)
5. Father, it doesn't matter whether I deserve it or not, I receive divine favour from You in the mighty name of Jesus (Proverbs 18:22)
6. Father, let the spirit of favour fall upon me now, in the mighty name of Jesus. (Genesis 6:8)
7. Father, bless me and make me great in the mighty name of Jesus. (Psalm 5:12a)
8. Father, as You blessed Abraham with divine favour, please bless me too in Jesus' name (Genesis 22:18)
9. Daddy, please grant me divine favour so that I can excel in the mighty name of Jesus. (Genesis 6:8)

10. Daddy, like Abraham, bless everyone that blesses me and curse everyone that curses me in the name of Jesus. (Genesis 12:3)

11. Daddy, like Abraham, bless many families through me in the name of Jesus. (Genesis 22:18)

12. Daddy, please do not let my blessings be transferred to my neighbour in the mighty name of Jesus. (Proverbs 11:25)

13. Father, let every step I take from this day lead to huge success and earth-shaking testimonies in the mighty name of Jesus. (Proverbs 3:6)

14. Daddy, establish my family and I as Your holy people in the name of Jesus. (Exodus 26:33)

15. Father, cause me to be fruitful and multiply in the mighty name of Jesus. (Genesis 1:28)

16. Father, open my family and I unto Your good Treasure in the name of Jesus. (Deuteronomy 28:11)

17. Father, my family and I receive Your goodness in this land in the mighty name of Jesus. (Psalm 27:13)

18. Father, according to Your word, I shall be head and not the tail in the mighty name of Jesus. (Deuteronomy 28:13)

19. Daddy, as I go out today, I ask for special favour from You in the mighty name of Jesus. (Isaiah 58:11)

20. Father, increase my faith that I may see Your favour in my life in Jesus' name (Luke 17:5)

21. Father, Your power is unlimited, and Your strength is endless, please fill my life with Your divine favour in the mighty name of Jesus. (Psalm 90:17)

22. Daddy, please let the entirety of my life reflect Your divine favour in the mighty name of Jesus. (Psalm 90:17)

23. Father, just as You favoured Esther before the King in the palace, please favour me as well in the mighty name of Jesus. (Esther 2:17)

24. Daddy, let every blessing and favour You have earmarked for me and my family not pass us by in the mighty name of Jesus. (Numbers 6:24-26)

25. Father, let the majesty of thy hands be the light that guides me, the compassion of the Son be the love that inspires me, and the presence of the Holy Spirit be the strength that empowers me in the mighty name of Jesus. (Psalm 139:10).

PRAYER FOR DIVINE VICTORY

Victory is part of your inheritance and identity in Christ Jesus. Having given your life to Jesus Christ, your victory is assured. Remember, Christ died to set you free from sin's bondage and penalty. As you walk through this pilgrim's journey, Christ will sure provide you the grace you need to be victorious.

I especially love Ephesians 6. It is easy for believers in Christ Jesus to forget who their real enemy is and end up fighting the wrong battles. The Scripture tells us:

For we do not wrestle against flesh and blood, but against principalities, against powers, against the rulers of the darkness of this age, against the spiritual host of wickedness in the heavenly places. (Ephesians 6:12 NKJV)

The Bible also tells us:

Yet in all these things we are more than conquerors through Him who loved us (Romans 8:37 NKJV).

If God says you are a victor, who can say otherwise? David was one such person that enjoyed several victories through obedience (1 Samuel 23:10-12).

Your victory is assured in Jesus. As written in 1 Corinthians 15:57 (NKJV):

But thanks be to God, who gives us the victory through our Lord Jesus Christ.

PRAYER POINTS:

1. Father, I thank you for giving me eternal victory in Christ Jesus through the gift of salvation. (Psalm 98:1)
2. Father, I thank you for the sacrifice of your son, Jesus Christ, which secured me and my family victory. (1 Corinthians 15:57)
3. Father, I receive boldness to fight and pursue in the mighty name of Jesus. (Deuteronomy 20:4)
4. Lord, thank you for your eternal victory over death and sin. (1 John 1:7)
5. Father, help me to walk in divine victory in Jesus' name. (Deuteronomy 20:4)
6. No weapon of Satan and his agents fashioned against me shall prosper, in the mighty name of Jesus. (Isaiah 54:17)
7. I declare that I have victory over all demonic oppressions in Jesus' name. (2 Thessalonians 3:3; Ephesians 6:10-11)

8. Father, please give me victory over every affliction in the mighty name of Jesus. (Psalm 34:19-20)

9. Father, deliver me and my household from every affliction of the devourer and surround me with the songs of deliverance in the mighty name of Jesus. (Psalm 32:7)

10. Father, deliver me from every affliction of sickness and disease in the mighty name of Jesus. (Psalm 34:4)

11. Father, deliver me from every affliction of heavy load and burden in the name of Jesus (Isaiah 22:25; Psalm 34:17)

12. Father, deliver me and my household from untimely death in the name of Jesus. (Psalm 118:17)

13. Father, let the blood of Jesus fight for me and grant me victory in Jesus' name. (Matthew 26:27-28)

14. Father, by the power in the blood of Jesus, I have power over sin, failures, delays, stagnation and poverty in the mighty name of Jesus. (Psalm 23:1-6)

15. Father, send your ministry of angels to fight for me in Jesus' name. (Psalm 91:11-12)

16. Father, do not let me or any member of my family become a victim of the Devil in Jesus' name. (Isaiah 54:17)

17. Daddy, please shut the mouth of every lion that has been sent from the pit of hell to devour me in the mighty name of Jesus. (Daniel 6:19-23)

18. Daddy, just as you tamed the lions and they obeyed Daniel, I ask that the laws of competition, business and marketplace will obey me and answer me in Jesus' name. (Daniel 6:19-23)

19. Just as Daniel came out of the lion's den unhurt, that I too will come out of life's battles victoriously and unscathed in the name of Jesus. (Daniel 6:23)

20. In the name that is above every other name, I decree that I shall be victorious in all my battles in Jesus' name. (Deuteronomy 20:4)

21. Father, by your power, I bind every strong man in my life trying to pull me down in the mighty name of Jesus. (Mark 3:27)

22. Oh Lord, let all my enemies be put to shame in the mighty name of Jesus. (Psalm 25:1)

23. Father, I nullify every power working against my destiny in the mighty name of Jesus. (Ephesians 2:10)

24. Father I loose myself from every satanic oppression against my life in the mighty name of Jesus. (Matthew 24:19)

25. Father, thank you for all the assurance of victories ahead in Jesus' name. (1 John 5:4; Deuteronomy 20:4)

PRAYER FOR DIVINE WISDOM AND DISCERNMENT

Recently, I have been calculating the worth of wisdom. Is it a lifetime's worth? What's so valuable about wisdom? If you had to choose between a bag full of silver or gold and a bag full of wisdom, which would you choose?

The Bible tells us of the richness of wisdom in Proverbs:

Blessed is the one who finds wisdom, and the one who gets understanding, for the gain from her is better than gain from silver and her profit better than gold. (Proverbs 3:14 ESV)

Wisdom is the principal thing; therefore, get wisdom: and with all thy getting get understanding. (Proverbs 4:7 KJV)

If any of you lack wisdom, let him ask of God that gives to all men liberally, and upbraided not, and it be given to him. (James 1:5 KJB)

The book of Proverbs extensively emphasizes the importance of wisdom. Paul, in most of his epistles to the New Testament churches, prayed for the people to receive the Spirit and workings of wisdom to maximize their potential.

Nothing is as important as walking in God's divine wisdom. By this, we are not referring to the human wisdom (Sophia) but that wisdom that comes from God almighty. So what is wisdom then?

Wisdom produces discernment, which is the ability and capacity to understand and perceive things by the Spirit of God. When we pray for God's wisdom, discernment, and guidance through the Holy Spirit, rest assured God will grant what we ask. He says if any of you lack wisdom, let him ask of God. The Bible tells us that He is our loving shepherd who will lead us to the path of righteousness, which ultimately leads to fulfillment and contentment.

The gift of discernment of spirits is one of the gifts of the Holy Spirit (1 Corinthians 12:4-11) and it is freely given divinely to advance the kingdom of God here on earth.

For the Lord gives wisdom; from His mouth come knowledge and understanding. (Proverbs 2:6 NIV)

PRAYER POINTS:

1. Father, Your word says in Proverbs that with wisdom comes long life. Father fill me with Your Spirit of wisdom so that I can fulfill my purpose in the name of Jesus.

2. Father, keep my eyes peeled so that I can see what my physical eyes cannot see in the name of Jesus. (Psalm 119:18)

3. Father, endue me with the Spirit of discernment today in the mighty name of Jesus. (Psalm 111:10)

4. O Lord, teach me Your way, that I may walk in Your wisdom in the mighty name of Jesus. (Psalm 86:11)

5. Daddy, according to Your Word, I ask that You fill me with the knowledge of Your will in all wisdom and discernment in the mighty name of Jesus. (Colossians 1:9)

6. Father, please open the eyes of my understanding and enlighten my heart that I may know the hope of Your calling and the riches of Your glorious inheritance in the saints in the mighty name of Jesus. (Ephesians 1:16)

7. From today, I shall no longer be blind spiritually, financially and relationally in Jesus' name. (Isaiah 42:6-7)

8. The Bible tells us in Luke 2:52 that Jesus grew in wisdom and stature. Daddy, please bless me with wisdom and help me to grow continuously in it and remain in it in Jesus' name. (Luke 2:52)

9. Father, please grant me wisdom that will unearth Your hidden treasures and help me to fear You and live in righteousness in the mighty name of Jesus. (Proverbs 2:3-5)

10. Father, help me to search for knowledge and discover Your divine treasure in the name of Jesus. (Proverbs 2:3-5)

11. Father, guide my path as I thirst for Your truths in the name of Jesus. (Proverbs 3:5-6)

12. Father, I am at a crossroads, and I don't know which way to turn. Please grant me clarity right now in the mighty name of Jesus. (Proverbs 2:3-5)

13. Father, help me to seek You always so that the plans that You have for my life may be successful. (Proverbs 15:1-2)

14. Lord, help me to become sensitive to Your Holy Spirit so that I can be wise and aligned to Your will in the mighty name of Jesus (Proverbs 15:1-2)

15. Dear Lord, reveal to me the things that will help lead a victorious and fruitful life in Jesus' name (James 1:5)

Let's consider Solomon's Prayer for Wisdom:

Now, Lord my God, you have made your servant king in place of my father David. But I am only a little child and do not know how to carry out my duties. Your servant is here among the people you have chosen, a great people, too numerous to count or number. So give your servant a discerning heart to govern your people and to distinguish between right and wrong. For who is able to govern this great people of yours? (1 Kings 3:7-9 NIV)

16. Father, I come in the same humility and sincerity of the heart as King Solomon. Please grant me wisdom as You did to him, in Jesus' name. (1 Kings 3:7-9)

17. Father, help me to trust You with my whole heart so I do not lean on my understanding, in Jesus' name. (Proverbs 3:3-5)

18. Father, please purify my fragile heart and grant me Your divine wisdom even as I make You the centre of my life in the mighty name of Jesus. (Ezekiel 36:25-27)

19. Father, by Your wisdom, guide me in all that I do, save me from hubris, arrogance, fear, and doubt in the mighty name of Jesus. (Psalm 25:4-5)
20. By the Spirit of God, I shall always know what to do at the right time in the name of Jesus. (Proverbs 2:6)

PRAYER FOR EXAM SUCCESS

In the Gospel of Matthew, the Scripture says:

But seek first his kingdom and righteousness, and all these things will be given to you as well. (Matthew 6:33 NIV)

Success in our exams and academic pursuits are a few of those add-ons the Lord promises to give us.

Exams and academic workloads can sometimes seem daunting and overwhelming, or perhaps impossible to get through. However, in our struggles at school, the Lord never fails us and never gives up on us.

As pressure and stress bear down on me, I find joy in your command. (Psalm 119:143 NLT)

I know the Lord is always with me. I will not be shaken, for he is right beside me. God also assures his children:

Even the youths shall faint and be weary, and the young men shall utterly fall: But those who wait on the lord shall renew their strength; they shall mount up with wings like eagles, they shall run and not be weary. They shall walk, and not faint. (Isaiah 40:30-31 NKJV)

Do not worry about anything, instead, pray about everything. Tell God what you need and thank him for all he has done so you can experience God's peace, which exceeds anything we can understand. (Philippians 4:6-7 NLT)

But blessed is the one who trusts in the Lord, whose confidence is in him. They will be like a tree planted by the water that sends out its roots by the stream. It does not fear when heat comes; its leaves are always green. It has no worries in a year of drought and never fails to bear fruit. (Jeremiah 17:7-8 NIV)

PRAYER POINTS:

1. Thank You for the gift of this institution and education. (1 Thessalonians 5:16)
2. Father, thank You for how far You have brought me in my academics. (2 Samuel 7:18)
3. Father, I pray that these exams would be a celebration of all I have learned in this season. (Psalm 121:2)
4. Father, please give me wisdom and discernment in the upcoming exams in Jesus' name. (Matthew 6:33)
5. Father, please help me to prioritize my workloads, tasks and schedules and grant me the grace to focus on what matters most and not major on minor. (Ecclesiastes 3:1; Matthew 6:33)
6. Father, strengthen me whenever I am weary (Deuteronomy 31:6)

7. Father, renew my spirit when I start to lose steam (Isaiah 40:31)

8. Father, help me to run the race to the finish line and end strong in the name of Jesus (2 Timothy 4:7)

9. Father, please make me an external excellency and the joy of many generations. (Isaiah 60:15)

10. Daddy, please help me to use my results and knowledge to advance Your kingdom here on earth, in the mighty name of Jesus. (1 Peter 4:10; Matthew 25:14-30)

11. Almighty God, grant me extravagant favour in the sight of my teachers, professors, and examiners. I put my trust in You, please lead me to success in the mighty name of Jesus. (Proverbs 16:3; 1 Kings 2:3)

12. The power of life and death is in the tongue, in the name that is above all other names, I decree and declare that I am victorious in this exam. (Proverbs 18:21)

13. For God has not given me a spirit of fear, but of power and of love and of sound mind. Father, as I study for and write this exam, dispel any anxiety and remove all apprehension in my life in Jesus' name. (2 Timothy 1:7)

14. Father, please fill me with divine wisdom and understanding and grant me speed in Jesus' name. (Exodus 28:3; 31:3, 26, 31)

15. Proverbs 21:31 says: *The horse is prepared for the day of battle, but deliverance is of the Lord.* Father grant me victory in Jesus' name.

16. In the name of Jesus, I banish every nervous feeling. Help me remember all that I have read. (Deuteronomy 8:2)

17. Father, sharpen my thinking, hone my understanding and help me to come out in a flying colour. (Proverbs 27:17)

18. Father, help me to remember everything that I need from my books and answer each question accurately in Jesus' name. (Proverbs 4:13)

19. As I take this exam, Father, please keep my mind alert and memory sharp in Jesus' name. (Luke 2:19; Deuteronomy 31:6)

20. Calm my nerves and help me concentrate in the mighty name of Jesus. (Psalm 121:1-2; Psalm 56:11)

21. Thank You Father because I know that my victory and success are guaranteed in Jesus' name. (1 Corinthians 10:13).

BREAKING YOKES, CURSES AND BARRIERS

It is crucial for believers to pray against curses and barriers in their walk with the Lord, as taught by Jesus Christ in His Sermon on the Mount.

Therefore, do not be anxious about tomorrow, for tomorrow will be anxious for itself. Sufficient unto the day is its own trouble. (Matthew 6:34 ESV)

The Scripture tells us that burden and yoke shall be taken off our necks:

And it shall come to pass in that day, that his burden will be taken away from your shoulder, and his yoke from off thy neck, and the yoke shall be destroyed because of the anointing oil (Isaiah 10:27 NKJV)

A yoke in its original meaning is referred to a harness made of wood by which two animals are tied together to pull a heavy load. However, that definition can be simplified to mean an unwanted burden placed upon someone's life by the devil. The result is coerced obedience and forced submission leading to servitude and can either be physical or spiritual or even both. To be yoked simply means to forcefully submit or surrender. A yoke could be in the form of bondage, strong limitation, stagnation, delay, unprofitable labour or even wicked programming.

Spiritual yokes usually act as strongholds hindering our progress and success. It is the worst form of struggle any child of God may experience along their pilgrim journey. There is a common stereotype that being a Christian is an easy thing. Yes, only by His grace. Brethren, come to this realization: for every level you go into in life, there will always be trials and temptations that you might not be prepared to tackle.

The world we are in requires us to be strong in the Lord and understand our authority in the Lord. Pray to always rely on the Word so it will work for you.

PRAYER POINTS:

1. Let the power in the blood of Jesus separate me from the sins of my ancestors in Jesus' name. (Exodus 20:5-6)
2. I release myself from any inherited bondage and limitation in the mighty name of Jesus. (Isaiah 11:1-5)
3. Father, send your axe of fire to the foundation of my life and destroy every yoke placed over my life. (Leviticus 21:5)

4. Break and loose me from every inherited evil curse. (Deuteronomy 5:6; 8:14)
5. Deliver me from all foundational strong men holding me captive. (Leviticus 19:28)
6. Father, free me from every wicked rod of the evil one rising against my family in Jesus' name. (Exodus 6:6)
7. Father, release me from every evil control and domination in Jesus' name. (Exodus 6:5)
8. Father, let the blood of Jesus remove any retrogressive label of failures, delay and loss placed over my life in Jesus' name (Deuteronomy 26:6; Joshua 24:17)
9. Lord, let the anointing of the Holy Spirit break me free from every yoke of stagnation in Jesus' name. (Judges 6:2-4)
10. Father, let every gate opened to the enemy by me or on my behalf by my parents, be closed forever in Jesus' name. (Isaiah 22:22)
11. My father and my God, please destroy every curse of poverty, failure and suffering in the mighty name of Jesus. (Luke 5:1-7; Exodus 1:11)
12. Daddy, heal my land and deliver me and my family from generational curses in Jesus' name. (Psalm 119:71)
13. For though we walk in the flesh, we do not war according to the flesh, for weapons of our warfare are not of the flesh, but divinely powerful for the destruction of fortresses. Father, give me a victory without a fight in the mighty name of Jesus. (2 Corinthians 10:3-4)
14. I rebuke every evil thought and negative word spoken against me and my family in Jesus' name. (Titus 1:10-11; Psalm 10:7)

15. Father, break every barrier that is hindering me from getting close to you in the mighty name of Jesus. (Isaiah 57:14; 1 Corinthians 8:9; 1 Thessalonians 2:10)

16. I curse every evil spirit in my life that attempts to obstruct my blessings. (Zechariah 4:7)

17. Father, every evil stronghold, let it vanish at the sound of Jesus' name. (Psalm 9:9)

18. For God has not given me the spirit of fear, but of power and love and of a sound mind. Father, in the name of Jesus I curse every spirit of fear and timidity in my life. (2 Timothy 1:7)

19. Holy Ghost fire, quench every arrow of prayerlessness fired at me by the devil in the name of Jesus. (Ephesians 6:6)

20. Anointing of the Holy Ghost, fall on me and break me from every yoke in the mighty name of Jesus. (Jeremiah 30:8; Isaiah 58:6)

21. Father, I thank you for answered prayers in Jesus' name I pray.

PRAYER FOR LIFE PARTNER

I truly believe that the knowledge of humanity passes through masculinity and femininity greatly so much so that we can't understand ourselves as man or woman separately if we don't have each other.

…and He brought her to the man. (Genesis 2:22 NKJV)

Jesus answered them,

*He created them male and female and blessed them. And He named them mankind. (*Genesis 5:2 NIV)

"Haven't you read," he replied, "that at the beginning the creator made them male and female?" (Matthew 19:4 NIV)

Have faith in God. I assure you that whoever tells this hill to get up and throw itself in the sea and does not doubt in his heart, but believes that what he says will happen, it will be done for him.

For this reason, I tell you: when you pray and ask for something, believe that you have received it, and you will be given whatever you ask for. (Mark 11:22-24 GNT)

When you are unmarried with no prospects in sight, you can easily spend most of your time in wishful thinking and fantasizing. It is easy to get so fixated on the type of person you want to spend the rest of your life with. As sweet as this may sound, only prayer can make it happen.

If you have been jilted in your past relationships, you probably would not want to open yourself up another time because you are afraid of what could happen. This has a propensity to pressure you into settling for a person that might not be the right person for you. You may worry that if you let the person go, you will never find anyone else to marry you in the future.

Nothing is too small or big to be taken to the Lord in prayer. It is important to pray into your future to continually enjoy God's presence.

And the Lord God said, it is not good that the man should be alone, I will make him an help meet for him. (Genesis 2:18 KJV)

Therefore, a man shall leave his father and his mother and shall cleave unto his wife: and they shall be one flesh. (Genesis 2:24 KJV)

Delight thyself also in the Lord; And he shall give thee the desires of your heart. (Psalm 37:4 NKJV)

It is important that a Christian marries a Christian. The Bible tells us in 2 Corinthians:

Do not be unequally yoked with unbelievers. For what partnership hs righteousness with lawlessness? Or what fellowship has light with darkness? (2 Corinthians 6:14 ESV)

Ladies, please avoid running after a man. Position yourself prayerfully and the man will come looking for you. The Bible says it is the man that does the searching and by so doing, you do not have to let off the aroma of desperation because you are looking for a soul mate thereby losing your self worth and self esteem. Not only ladies, even our young men also need to prayerfully conduct the searching and must be upright and beyond reproach.

Proverbs 18:22 says he that finds a wife finds a good thing and obtains favour from the Lord.

The Scripture also says:

Daughters of Jerusalem, I charge you: Do not arouse or awaken love until it so desires. (Song of Solomon 8:4 NIV)

Beloved child of God, let us not join the world in changing the Lord's order. It is the man that finds the woman and not vice versa. If God reveals the man to you before the man talks to you, do not go to him directly. Ask God to reveal the same to him and you can as well talk to your pastor about it for guidance. Don't go to him and say, "God said you are my husband." That's an aberration. Do not allow pressure to coerce you into disobeying God's principle. His timing is the best. Though finding your life partner may tarry, wait for it, it will surely come, and you will be glad you did.

Focus on building a genuine relationship with God first and foremost and lines will fall into pleasant places for you. Remember, it is purpose that gives value to everything in life and marriage is a commitment that lasts a lifetime. The late Dr. Myles Munroe has an incredible teaching on preparation for marriage called the Myth of Singleness. Find it and read it and it will bless your soul.

An excellent wife who can find? She is far more precious than jewels. The heart of her husband trusts in her, and he will have no lack of gain. She does him good, and not harm, all the days of her life. (Proverbs 31:10-12 ESV)

PRAYER POINTS:

1. Father, I thank You for daily loading me with benefits. (Psalm 68:19)
2. Father, Your Word says that those that wait upon the Lord shall renew their strength. Help me to wait on You. (Isaiah 40:31)
3. Daddy, teach me to wait on You. (Isaiah 40:31)
4. Father, do not let me fall into the arms of the wrong person in the name of marriage in the mighty name of Jesus. (Psalm 37:4; Malachi 2:16)
5. Father, bring my loneliness to an end in the mighty name of Jesus. (Genesis 2:18)
6. Dear Lord, as I wait, please prepare me to be the best spouse that I can be. (Psalm 27:14)

7. Father, connect me with the bone of my bone and let Your will be done in my life in the mighty name of Jesus. (Genesis 2:23)

8. Father, grant me grace to to discover and follow Your perfect will for me concerning my life's partner in the mighty name of Jesus. (Roman 12:1-2)

9. Father, please reveal to me the flaws in my life and send the Holy Spirit to help me work on those flaws in the mighty name of Jesus. (1 Corinthians 2:10)

10. Father, as You prepare me to be a worthy companion to my future spouse, please go ahead and prepare them in the mighty name of Jesus. (Genesis 2:18)

11. Father, do not let me make a wrong choice in my marriage in Jesus name. (Psalm 37:4)

12. Father, I sever all ties and separate myself from every ungodly partner in the mighty name of Jesus (2 CorinthiansCorinthians 6:14-18)

13. Father, satisfy me early in life. Father, let my partner show up at Your timing in Jesus' name. (Psalm 189:16)

14. Lord, Your time is perfect. May I not be swayed by my own wisdom. Help me to put my trust in You always while I wait on Your timing in the mighty name of Jesus. (Psalm 27:14)

15. Father, let my day of joy come quickly in the mighty name of Jesus. (Psalm 30:5)

16. Father, help me to discern Your will concerning who to marry in Jesus name. (Psalm 25:4-5)

17. Dear Lord, give me the discernment to be able to recognize and pick out the good voice from the crowd of voices that will seek my hands in marriage (James 1:17)

18. The Bible says that every good and perfect gift comes from God. Father, grant me a perfect and sweet marriage in the mighty name of Jesus. (1 Corinthians 13:4-8; Proverbs 31:10-31)

19. Father, from today forward, let everything begin to work for my good in marriage in the name of Jesus. (Romans 8:28)

20. Father, bless my marriage and cause it to be fruitful even here on earth in Jesus' name (Genesis 28:6)

21. Father, bless my union with wonderful children and help me to be submissive to my future partner in the mighty name of Jesus. (Genesis 1:28)

22. As a woman, Father, let me not struggle with submission. Holy Spirit please help me to submit with ease to my future husband in Jesus' name. (Ephesians 5:22)

23. As a man, Father, let me not struggle to love my wife as Christ loves the church. Holy Spirit help me to speak the love language that my future wife understands in the mighty name of Jesus. (Ephesians 5:25)

PRAYER FOR SPIRITUAL AWAKENING

This is all the more urgent, for you know how late it is; time is running out. Wake up, for our salvation is nearer now than when we first believed. (Roman 13:11 NLT)

Therefore, let us not sleep, as do others, but let us watch and be sober. (1 Thessalonians 5:6 KJB)

The Bible warns of dangers of spiritual sleep or drowsiness. Sleep is often used figuratively to express death (John 11:11-13), spiritual drowsiness or lukewarmness (Ephesians 5:14). The Bible exhorts believers to wake up, to be revived and stay revived.

Revival is not a trivial idea. We need to get revived and stay revived. Apostle Paul wrote to the congregation of fledgling believers in Christ at the heart of the Roman empire admonishing them in the doctrine of faith, how they ought to love one another and live out all aspects of their life.

Let's look at Paul's charge in another version:

And do this, understanding the present time. The hour has come for you to wake up from your slumber, because our salvation is nearer now than when we first believed. (Roman 13:11 NIV)

The Bible also refers to a figurative character in the book of Proverbs:

"How long will you slumber, O sluggard. When will you rise from your sleep?" (Proverbs 6:9 NKJV)

Prophet Isaiah told the sleeping and sleepy Israel:

Arise, shine, for thy light has come and the glory of the Lord is risen upon you. (Isaiah 60:1 NIV)

One would think that God was done talking to mankind about waking up from sleep, but Jesus went even further in Matthew 25:26 to address the sleeping servant.

But the master replied, 'You wicked and lazy servant!' (Matthew 25:26 NLT)

The subject of spiritual awakening covers a special spectrum of Christian living and the Bible unambiguously warns us to stay awake because we do not know the hour nor the day when the Son of Man shall come like a thief.

There is a nexus between spiritual drowsiness by Christians, the church and society's debauchery and downward spiral culminating in the growing moral decadence prevalent in our generation. You may recall that Americans saw prayer taken out of schools in 1962. And how abortion was legalized in 1973.

Just a few years ago, same sex marriage started gaining ground to the point where a case involving a Christian business baker was litigated in the United States Supreme court for their refusal to make a cake for a gay wedding. Thank God for that little court victory. These are just a handful of examples showing how spiritual sleep has crept in over time.

Before anyone can engage with God in prayer, they must bring themselves under the purview of God's Word and examine themselves. The good news is, God assures mankind in 2 Chronicles 7:14

If my people, which are called by my name, shall humble themselves, and pray, and seek my face, and turn from their wicked ways; then will I hear from heaven, and will forgive their sin, and will heal their land.

PRAYER POINTS:

1. Father, I thank You for what You are doing in my life and in Your church. (1 Thessalonians 5:16-18)
2. Father, thank You for Your amazing grace and power (2 Corinthians 13:14)
3. Dear Lord, please forgive me and Your church for drifting away from You and for allowing ourselves to be taken in by the offerings of this world in Jesus name. (2 Chronicle 7:14)

4. Father, create in me a clean heart and set me on fire again for the work ahead of me in Jesus name (Psalm 51:10)

5. Father, transform my heart and release a fresh fire upon my prayer altar (Psalm 51:10)

6. Father, give me the grace to travail in the place of prayer. (Psalm 63:1)

7. Holy Father, grant me and Your church, a burning hunger for Your work and a passion for fervent prayer in Jesus' name. (Matthew 5:6)

8. Father, revive me. Revive my spirit, body and soul. (Psalm 85:6)

9. Father, bestow on me a fresh spiritual hunger. (Romans 9:1-3)

10. Daddy, please let flames of Your spirit consume my heart. (Isaiah 44:3)

11. Lord, revive the church and pour out Your Spirit onto the church by Your mercy. (Habakkuk 3:2)

12. Lord, I want more of You and let Your revival be powerfully ignited in my heart in Jesus' name. (Psalm 143:6)

13. Righteous God, please send an overwhelming conviction of sin, revelation of inner brokenness and genuine repentance upon Your church today in the mighty name of Jesus. (Psalm 51:17; Proverbs 28:13; 2 Corinthians 7:1,10)

14. Father, help me and Your church to draw near to You and seek You with all our hearts in Jesus name. (Jeremiah 29:13)

15. Father, cause Your church and pastors to come to You in true repentance, contriteness of heart and brokenness in the mighty name of Jesus. (Isaiah 57:15; Matthew 26:39)

16. Righteous God, purify the hearts and minds of Your people so that our thoughts are always turned toward You in the mighty name of Jesus. (Psalm 86:11-13)

17. Father, please revive the hearts of all believers especially those who have left their first love in the mighty name of Jesus. (2 Chronicles 16:9)

18. Lord God, draw me and Your church back into a right relationship with You in Jesus name. (James 4:8)

19. Righteous God, bestow on me fresh burdens and care for the loss souls in the mighty name of Jesus. (Psalm 126:6)

20. Dear Lord, please wake me up! Remind me to live aware and redeem any lost time in the mighty name of Jesus. Help Your church to be wise to redeem the time in Jesus' name. (Ephesians 5:16)

PRAYERS THAT ARE PROPHETIC DECLARATIONS

The Bible tells us,

Thou shall also decree a thing, and it shall be established unto thee: and the light shall shine upon thy ways. When men are cast down, then thou shall say, There is lifting up; and he shall save the humble person. (Job 22:28-29 KJV)

There's so much power in the words we speak and what we say today creates our tomorrow. If we want a healthy and prosperous tomorrow, then we should be applying wisdom in speaking words that bring positive outcomes because the future depends on it. Declaring the Word of God simply means to make known, to affirm or to state authoritatively.

In Genesis, God spoke and declared all things into existence. Since we are created in God's image, consequently, he has given us the authority and power to declare over our lives. Sometimes, we might be declaring over our life without even knowing it. Have you ever said to your self, "I hate my life," or "My life isn't sweet," or "I'm finished" or "I'm so fat and ugly," or "I am in trouble." All these are negative declarations that could bring sad and painful outcomes into our lives. How do I know? I have been there and over time, I have learned that what I say or what I think brings what I am focusing on into my life.

Therefore, whatever you do not want, you have the authority to reject it and whatever you desire you have the authority to speak it into existence. The Bible makes it clear that with our mouth, we can have whatsoever we say we want. Our tongue is a weapon and remember, a closed mouth is a closed destiny.

In addition, we must learn to fill in our names in some Bible stories because God's Word is intended to be a personal gift to us. The Bible tells us that He knows us by name and can handle all our needs. Personalizing scriptural truths helps us understand that the Bible isn't just a storybook or a collection of divine fables. Always declare who you are in Jesus Christ.

DECLARATIVE PRAYER POINTS:

1. I am (Insert your name here), Lord, you know me by name.
2. I am a child of God
3. I am redeemed from the hand of the enemy
4. I am forgiven
5. I am saved by Grace through faith

6. I am justified and sanctified
7. I am a new creation in Christ Jesus
8. I am a partaker of God's divine nature
9. I am redeemed from the curse of the law
10. I am delivered from the powers of darkness
11. I am being led by the Holy Spirit
12. I am kept in safety wherever I go
13. I have the divine favour of God in whatever I do today and always
14. I have the divine favour of God wherever I go today in Jesus name
15. I am getting all my needs met by Jesus Christ
16. I am casting all my cares upon Jesus
17. I am doing all things through Christ who strengthens me
18. I am an heir to the blessings of Abraham
19. I am an heir to eternal life
20. My going out is blessed; my coming in is blessed as well.
21. I am exercising my authority over the enemy
22. I am above only and not beneath
23. I am the head and not the tail
24. I am more than a conqueror
25. I am living out God's Word for my life
26. I am establishing God's Word here on earth
27. I overcome by the blood of the Lamb and the word of my testimony
28. I am daily overcoming the devil
29. I am not moved by what I see; I am not moved by what I feel
30. I am walking by faith and not by sight
31. I am casting down every vain imagination

32. I am bringing every thought into captivity in Christ Jesus
33. I am being transformed by the renewing of my mind
34. I am a co-labourer together with God
35. I am the righteousness of God through Christ
36. I am the light of the world
37. I am blessing the Lord always and will continue praising Him with my mouth
38. I am putting on the mind of Jesus Christ
39. I am a continuous blessing to my brothers, sisters, colleagues, and brethren in Christ Jesus
40. I am free from all bondage because the Holy Spirit dwells inside of me

PRAYERS DECLARING HEALING

And suddenly, a woman who had a flow of blood for twelve years came from behind and touched the hem of His garment. For she said to herself, "If only I may touch His garment, I shall be made well." But Jesus turned around, and when He saw her, He said, "Be of good cheer, daughter; your faith had made you well." And the woman was made well from that hour. (Matthew 9:20-22 NKJV)

The Bible says in Isaiah:

But He was wounded for our transgressions, He was bruised for our iniquities. The chastisement for our peace was upon Him, and by His stripes we are healed. (Isaiah 53:5 NKJV)

The Bible tells us our bodies are the temple of God. Recent events, particularly the global COVID-19 pandemic, has sent millions of people around the world to an early grave.

But it is important that we understand who we are in Christ so we can scripturally declare healing to our bodies.

PRAYER POINTS:

1. Jesus Christ has redeemed me from the curse of the law. Therefore, I forbid any sickness or disease to come upon my body. (1 Peter 2:24)
2. Every disease or virus that touches my body dies instantly in the name of Jesus. (Matthew 15:13; Mark 11:23; Proverbs 14:30)
3. I declare that every cell, organ, and tissue in my body functions in the perfection to which God created it to function. (Psalm 139:13-14)
4. I forbid any malfunction in my cells, tissues, and organs in the mighty name of Jesus (Psalm 139:13-14)
5. I am healed by the stripes of Jesus. (Isaiah 53:5)
6. I am delivered from the power sickness and diseases. I am delivered of COVID-19, flu, cancer, HIV, pains (name the sickness here) in the mighty name of Jesus. (Exodus 23:25)
7. I am exercising my authority over COVID-19, headaches, pain, fever etc. in the name of Jesus. (Luke 10:19)
8. Heavenly Father, through your Word you have imparted your life into me. That life restores my body with every breath I breathe and every word I speak in the name of Jesus. (Jeremiah 30:17)
9. Father, Your Word has become a part of me and therefore, it is flowing in my bloodstream cleansing me from every disorder, sickness and disease from my cells, tissues, and organs. (Matthew 10:1-8)

10. The Blood of Jesus is restoring and transforming my health in the name of Jesus. (Jeremiah 30:17)

11. Father, Your Word has become flesh; for You sent Your Word and healed me in the mighty name of Jesus. (Psalm 107:20)

12. Father, You raised Jesus Christ from the dead and He dwells in me, permeating His life through my body and sending healing to my entire body. (Romans 8:11)

13. Dear Lord, let every cell, tissue, organ that does not promote health in my body be yanked from its source. (Exodus 23:25; 2 Corinthians 4:10-11)

14. Father, by Your mercy, I forbid my immune system from allowing tumours or growths to live in my body in the mighty name of Jesus. (Revelation 21:4)

15. My body is the temple of Your Holy Spirit. (1 Corinthians 6:19-20)

16. I decree that my body is in perfect chemical condition. My pancreas secretes the right amount of hormones, insulin for life and health in the mighty name of Jesus. (3 John 1:2)

17. In the name of Jesus, I stand and I speak to my bones, joints, and muscles to function properly in the mighty name of Jesus. (Ephesians 4:16)

18. *He carried away our sins in His own body on the cross so we can be dead to sin and live for what is right. I have been healed by His wounds.* (1 Peter 2:24) Today, in the name of Jesus, let God's promises permeates every joint, bone, marrow and muscle of my body.

19. In the name of Jesus, from today, I give no place to sickness, disease, or pain. For God sent His Word and healed me. (Psalm 107:20)

20. Heavenly Father, your Word says those who hope in you will renew their strength. They will soar on wings like eagles; they will run and not grow weary; and will walk and not faith. Father, please keep me healthy and strong so that I may continue to labour in your vineyard in the mighty name of Jesus. (Isaiah 40:31)

PRAYER FOR CHURCH GROWTH

I've been privileged to fellowship with Redeemed Christian Church of God churches in Nigeria, United Kingdom, United States and Canada. In all my experiences, they have one thing is common: prayers are usually Bible-based and strongly rooted in God's Word. I truly desire to see the church universal continue to declare God's Word undiluted.

The Bible says:

And the remnant who have escaped of the house of Judah shall again take root downward, and bear fruit upward. (2 Kings 19:30)

Only the Word of God can bring true emancipation from the world especially in the wake of the ongoing global pandemic that has run us ragged and left the world at its wit's end.

The Bible says:

Behold, how good and how pleasant it is for brethren to dwell together in unity! It is like the precious ointment upon the head, that ran down upon the beard, even Aaron's beard: that went down to the skirts of his garments; As the dew of Hermon, and as the dew that descended upon the mountains of Zion: for there the Lord commanded the blessing, even life for evermore. (Psalm 133:1–3 KJV)

The body of Christ needs to stay united to pray united to get results. The body of Christ must endeavour to do the following:

to speak evil of no one, to avoid quarrelling, to be gentle, and to show perfect courtesy toward all people. (Titus 3:2 ESV)

Be alert and of sober mind. Your enemy the devil prowls around like a roaring lion looking for someone to devour. (1 Peter 5:8 NIV)

Brethren, often, the devil's prime target is the Church of God around the world. One of the ways the devil does this is by attempting to hinder the testimony of believers and the other way is by striking the shepherds. Therefore, it's important that we continue to pray for the church.

PRAYER POINTS:

1. Father Lord, please inspire the church to utilize its spiritual gifts to serve one another (1 Peter 4:10-12)
2. *And they devoted themselves to the apostles' teaching and the fellowship, to the breaking of bread and the prayers. (Acts 2:42)* Father, unify your church through your body in Jesus' name.

3. Father, Your Word says we should continue steadfastly in prayer, being watchful in it with thanksgiving. Father, please send Your Holy Spirit to help the church to remain watchful in prayer. (Colossians 4:2)

4. Father, end every opposition to the church in the mighty name of Jesus. (Titus 2:7-8)

5. Father, bring an end to every form of schism in the body of Christ. (1 Corinthians 1:10)

6. Father, I nullify every evil plan of the enemy against Your church in the name of Jesus. (Ephesians 6:12)

7. I reject every negative and fake anointing on any of our members in Jesus' name. (Matthew 7:21-23)

8. I declare divine insurance for all our members against failure, loss, accident, and premature death in the mighty name of Jesus. (Luke 5:5-7)

9. I cancel every power working against the vision of Christ Jesus in our church in Jesus' name. (Numbers 12:6)

10. Father, please send Your reaper angels to the harvest field to destroy every work of Satan against your church in Jesus' name. (1 John 3:8)

11. I release every of our members from any inherited bondage in the mighty name of Jesus. (Romans 8:21)

12. Father, I pray that the church today would have a greater love for the lost sheep. (John 15:13)

13. I pray for the spirit of wisdom and revelation to rest upon the church. (Ephesians 1:15-21)

14. I pray that the eyes of every member of your church be opened. (Matthew 6:22)

15. Father, protect the church from every form of error and pride in Jesus' name. (John 17:15)

16. Father, I pray that hunger and passion for lost souls would be restored to the church in Jesus' name. (Luke 15:1-7)

17. Dear Lord, I pray that the church would seek Your face like never before in Jesus' name. (Psalm 27:8)

18. Father, fill your church with the spirit of love and unity among believers so they may love one another in Jesus' name. (1 Corinthians 1:10)

19. Father, rend the heavens and level every mountain standing against your church in Jesus' name. (Isaiah 64:1)

20. Father, your word says you shall speak to them in your wrath and vex them in your sore displeasure. Father, put an end to all the laws that oppress the poor and make mockery of your Word in the nations of the world. Lord, vex them in your sore displeasure in the name of Jesus. (Psalm 2:5)

21. Father, let heaven open over your church always in the mighty name of Jesus. The church shall not operate under a closed heaven in Jesus' name. (Revelation 19:11)

22. Father, please let your Presence go with the church and let it be mighty and heavy in Jesus' name. (Exodus 33:15)

23. Upon this rock I will build my church and the gates of Hades shall not prevail against the church. Father, let nothing prevail against your church in Jesus' name. (Matthew 16:18)

PRAYER FOR THE PASTOR

When I was a teenager, I heard this line from a William Shakespeare play:

"Uneasy lies the head that wears the crown."

Nearly every issue in the church hangs over the head of the pastor. Being a leader is a blessing from God and with that blessing comes great responsibilities. The Bible tells us that God is interested in who leads his people – both in the spiritual and in the secular. Some people do not consider it appropriate to pray for their political leaders. This thinking is not in sync with the Word of God. The Scripture encourages believers to pray for leaders across all strata.

In 1 Timothy 1:1-4, the Bible says:

I urge, then, first, that petitions, prayers, intercession, and thanksgiving be made for all people – for kings and all those in authority, that we may live peaceful and quiet lives in all godliness and holiness. This is good, and pleases God our saviour, who wants all people to be saved and to come to a knowledge of the truth. (1 Timothy 2:1-4 NIV)

At the other end of the spectrum, it is often easy for folks to assume that our pastors are super humans, super Christians or super firebrands that cannot falter. However, pastors are mere humans and are faced daily with same temptations as any normal person. One of the most important prayers anyone can offer is God's protection over their shepherd.

Then I will give you a shepherd after my own heart, who will lead you with knowledge and understanding. (Jeremiah 3:15 NIV)

Pastors are usually the enemy's principal target and if there is a crack in the lead armoury, then the sheep may scatter. Pastors need prayers to stay the course as sometimes the purpose of their calling gets lost in the shuffle of their daily lives.

PRAYER POINTS:

1. Father, thank You for sending my pastor to shepherd the church. (Jeremiah 3:15)
2. Thank You, Lord, for the measure of Your grace upon my pastor. (Numbers 6:24-26)
3. Holy Spirit, help my pastor to serve you and truly desire you. (Deuteronomy 6:5)
4. Father, show my pastor the way in the mighty name of Jesus. (Proverbs 3:5-6)
5. Father, show mercy on my pastor. (2 Samuel 24:14)

6. Father, renew the strength of my pastor with your energy. (Isaiah 40:31)
7. Daddy, please do not let my pastor throw in the towel. (Galatians 6:9)
8. Father, give my pastors blinders so they can stay keenly focused on You and Your purposes only in the mighty name of Jesus. (Galatians 6:9)
9. Dear Lord, increase my pastor in wisdom. (James 1:5-6)
10. Lord, please do not let the enemy strike my pastor. (Matthew 26:31)
11. Father, keep our pastor (shepherd) in the right place so we (sheep) may not be scattered. (Matthew 26:31)
12. Father, lead my pastor not into temptation and protect them from evil. (Psalm 23)
13. Daddy, may my pastor's walk with you be filled with patience and may their footsteps bring peace and joy to every home in the mighty name of Jesus. (Ephesians 4:2)
14. Daddy, preserve my pastors and their family in Jesus' name.
15. Daddy, please preserve my pastor's marriage and keep it strong as a model of Jesus' relationship with the church. (Ephesians 5:25)
16. Daddy, let the bond between my pastor and their spouse grow stronger than ever before. (Ephesians 5:25)
17. Daddy, please build a hedge of protection around my pastor's marriage. (Matthew 19:6)
18. Father, please always reveal your will to my pastor and raise them up after your own heart. (1 Peter 2:15)
19. Father may your gospel not be tainted by greed in the life of my pastor in Jesus' name. (1 Peter 5:1-4)

20. Daddy, help my pastor to truly love you with all their heart, spirit, soul and body. (1 Timothy 1:5)
21. Daddy, please nourish my pastor's soul and spirit with Your word in secret place. (2 Timothy 2:15)
22. Father, allow my pastor to glory only in the cross in the mighty name of Jesus. (Galatians 6:14)
23. Dear Lord, keep my pastor from the traditions of men and religion which hold the form of godliness but deny its power. (1 Timothy 2:3)
24. Father, let my pastor's messages and teachings always be in synergy with the Holy Spirit in the mighty name of Jesus. (Colossians 2:18)
25. Dear Lord, heal my pastor of any hurt or abuse they have suffered during their walk with you in the mighty name of Jesus. (Isaiah 61:3)

SPECIAL PRAYERS

---

1. SPECIAL PRAYER FOR THE CHILDREN

Prayer has the propensity to destroy the plans of the evil one to capture the hearts of our children. The Word of God tells us:

The reason the Son of God appeared was to destroy the devil's work. (1 John 3:8 NIV)

A lot is at stake here, and we must passionately protect our children through prayer.

Say this prayer:

"Father, thank You for Your son, Jesus, whose sacrifice made it possible for me to have direct communication with You. What a life-changing privilege and what an honour! This is the confidence we have in You: that if we ask anything according to Your will, You will hear us. Thank You for the gift of the Holy Spirit that helps us to commune with You intimately.

I reject every seed of Satan in the lives of our children. I bind every old spirit hounding our children. Let every cord of sin be broken and shattered. Let every fragmented soul of our children that belongs to You come to them right now in the name of Jesus. I sever every tie to our children that doesn't give them the leeway to serve You. I break the tie of ritual abuse in the life of our children. I bind every old spirit and every sin that has come to torment our children. Cleanse our children from every form of satanic confirmation, sexual addiction, any involvement in occultism, satanic bible, curses of sodomy and witchcraft symbolism. I renounce and break the seal of Satan, the pentagram on the forehead, the golden triangle and its opening of the psychic third eye. Father cleanse them from every dimension of the third eye. Father, close every psychic entry point in Jesus' name. I renounce and smash every twisted horn of evil gods and break their power over our children. I break off every dementia fragmentation of the mind, schizophrenia, personality disorder in our children, as well as in our family line in the mighty name of Jesus.

I break the power of every water spirit, masturbation, wrong sexuality and strange orientation. I renounce and break every foul spirit, every cloven foot, and every effort to be terrorized by demons. I renounce every attempt by Satan to cause misogyny, I renounce every attempt by Satan to stir up the spirit of feminism and male chauvinism that comes from the pit of hades. I renounce and break every spirit of prostitution that comes with pornography and temple prostitution in the lives of our young men and women. I cancel every hatred of men and women. I nullify every spirit of lesbianism, gay lifestyle, and homosexuality. I submit to You Lord, take away every ungodliness and end time perversion in the lives of our children. I bind every spirit of witchcraft, wizardry, sodomy, sexual perversion, Jezebel and satanic ritual consummation. I decree and declare that every evil spirit leave our children alone in the mighty name of Jesus.

I sever the ties of every bad and nefarious relationship that our children may be involved in right now in Jesus' name. I renounce and break every Absolomic spirit, the spirit of rebellion and mutiny in the lives of our children. I bind and cast out every spirit of fear, doubt, anger, hatred, greed, envy, hubris, pride, ego, unhealthy competition, seduction, antichrist, robbery, thievery, pretense, and ignorance. I renounce them right now in the mighty name of Jesus. In the name of Jesus Christ of Nazareth, loose them and let them go in Jesus' mighty name I have prayed. Amen"

2. SPECIAL PRAYER FOR STORMY MARRIAGE

I will give you a marriage analogy using a garden. Sometimes a garden can still look fine on first glance, but the plants are dead on the inside. They just haven't fallen over yet. Marriages can get that way too. They look fine on the outside, but within, they are dead. Whenever the man or wife sees the pastor or any member of the church, they pretend that all is well. This does not fulfill God's plan for our lives, and it certainly doesn't glorify Him.

Say this prayer or adjust it to fit for purpose:

"Father, I pray for anyone reading this book whose marriage garden is going through any form of storm. I ask in the name that is above every other name: receive fresh seeds upon Your marriage garden, fresh fire upon Your marriage altar and fresh whispers of love. Receive fresh breath, fresh wine and fresh flowers in Your marriage garden in the mighty name of Jesus.

"I lift up any marriage garden experiencing storms of mistrust, storms of infidelity, storms of lack, storms of illness, storms of failures and delays, and storms of fruitlessness. In the name of Jesus, I join my faith and decree and declare peace. Any marriage garden that looks good on the outside, but dead on the inside, I stand upon the higher priestly rod and I decree and declare, return to Your original point. Return to where the marriage was on the wedding night in the name of Jesus. From today, receive a harvest of love, trust, joy and fulfillment in the mighty name of Jesus. Father, help husbands and wives appreciate their differences and show them brand new areas where they complement each other. Give them fresh eyes to admire each other. From today, receive fresh seeds of love in Your marriage, seeds of fidelity, seeds of respect and dignity, seeds of time and seeds of communication so You can spend quality time together. Thank You, Lord Jesus, for the assurance that You have answered my prayer in Jesus mighty name I pray. Amen."

3. SPECIAL PRAYER AGAINST PREMATURE & UNTIMELY DEATH

I will reward them with long life; I will save them. (Psalm 91:16 GNT)

I shall not die, but live, and declare the works of the Lord. (Psalm 118:17 NKJV)

God created man to fulfill their destiny on earth. In Psalm 8 and Hebrews 2:6-8, God reveals His purpose as originally ordained in Genesis 1:26-30. But the cemetery is full of unfulfilled destinies cut short from the original purpose of God. That will not be the portion of anyone reading this book in the mighty name of Jesus.

Say this prayer:

"Father Lord, in the name of Jesus thwart every plan and operation of the wicked one against my life or the lives of any of my family members. Dear Lord, any attack on my life or destiny is cancelled now in the name of Jesus. Father, I take divine immunity for my life, I take divine immunity for the lives of my spouse and children. I inoculate my life and the lives of my children with the blood of Jesus. No instruments and arrows of death will touch us in Jesus' name. Father, please by the greatness of Your power, preserve my life and the lives of everyone in this home who have been appointed to die prematurely in Jesus' name. I cancel every premature and untimely death hanging over anyone in this house in the name of Jesus. Dear Lord, by Your mercies, please lift me and my family members out from the gates of death and redeem our souls from the power of the grave in the mighty name of Jesus. We will live and not die until we fulfill our divine purpose in the mighty name of Jesus. Thank You, Lord, for answer prayers in Jesus mighty name I have prayed."

4. SPECIAL PRAYER FOR EXPECTANT MOTHERS

Writing this book gives away one of my nuggets. Praying for women waiting for the fruit of the womb is one of the most important areas that I am passionate about. It is my hidden ministry and no testimony gladdens my heart as a woman who has been blessed with a fruit of the womb after waiting to conceive. I can easily relate with what a woman who is waiting on the Lord goes through in a typical day. They truly deserve prayer of intercession from the saints.

The Bible says:

So, God created man in his own image, in the image of God created he him; male and female created he them. And God blessed them, and God said unto them, Be fruitful, and multiply, and replenish the earth, and subdue it. (Genesis 1:27-28a)

The original plan of God as contained in Genesis is to fill the earth and that plan has not changed. I believe that in every woman there is a longing to do what she was created to do. I know that a woman's metabolism, anatomy and physiology are wired for bearing children. Her arms were made to hold a child, and she can feel empty when she is denied that privilege. Even female celebrities, female politicians and women in sports or women who for one reason or another have chosen not to have children still experience pangs of desire to hold a child in their arms from time to time. For women who very much want their own children and have been denied that experience, there's a pain so deep that only God can soothe. The Bible says in Proverbs 30:15-16 the barren womb is never satisfied.

The Bible tells us:

Children are a heritage from the Lord, offspring a reward from him. Like arrows in the hands of a warrior are children born in one's youth. Blessed is the man whose quiver is full of them. They will not be put to shame when they contend with their opponents in court. (Psalm 127:3-5 NIV)

If you are a woman or man and you have been waiting on the Lord for this blessing, I want to reassure you and your spouse of God's faithfulness. Jesus the same yesterday, today and forever (Hebrews 13:8). Continue to do all the right thing and keep holding on to His promises and be strong in the Lord because the vision is yet for an appointed time.

For the vision is yet for an appointed time; but at the end it will speak, and it will not lie. Though it tarries, wait for it; because it will surely come, it will not tarry. (Habakkuk 2:3 NKJV)

If you are a wife and would like to be a mother, to hold your own babies in your hands, please join your faith with that of your spouse now – physically join your hands as well if you can – because there is power in the prayer of unity.

The Bible says:

Again, truly I tell you that if two of you on earth agree about anything they ask for, it will be done for them by my Father in heaven. (Matthew 18:19 NIV)

Nothing compares with two partners praying in unity.

Today, I join my faith with yours and together we agree as children of God and decree and declare that every broken or damaged cell or tissue or organ in any part of the body resulting in delay, is healed in the name of Jesus. Receive your healing and be fruitful in the mighty name of Jesus.

Say this prayer:

"Dear Father, I thank You because You are not a man that You should lie, neither a son of man that should change Your mind (Numbers 23:19), from the depth of my heart, I pray for my womb and all the wombs of every expectant mother.

Dear Father, I come by the rod of higher priesthood, and by the privilege of the election of grace, I invoke the angelic right now and I command wombs to open in the mighty name of Jesus. Lord, I know that a woman represents a gate therefore, I decree and declare, gates be opened now in the name of Jesus. I curse every barren womb. O ye barren womb, listen to the voice of the Lord, I curse you right now and I subject you under God's judgment in the mighty name of Jesus. The Bible says whatever we bind on earth is bound in heaven and whatever we loose on earth is loosed in heaven. Therefore, I bind every evil force behind this delay in conception and fruitlessness in the mighty name of Jesus. Father, please send your reaper angels to go to the harvest field right now. Destroy all the devices of the enemy so their hands can no longer perform any enterprise over my womb as well the womb of other daughters of Yours who are going through the same experience in the mighty name of Jesus.

I prophesy to my womb and to all my fellow expectant mothers and I declare you will bring forth your miracle babies in the mighty name of Jesus. I pray by the power of the Holy Spirit, to give us double blessings. As it pleases you Lord, please bless us with twins, triplets or quadruplets, and let the years that the locusts, caterpillars, cankerworms and palmerworms have eaten be restored back to your children in the mighty name of Jesus. Father, put every Peninnah that has been mocking me to shame in the name of Jesus. If there are prognoses which are medically bad concerning my case, I decree they are cancelled and declared null and void in the name of Jesus. Every unprofitable mark of fruitfulness and delays in my life, is hereby erased in the mighty name of Jesus.

Father, I annul every negative counsel on my life, and I destroy long time obstacles, long-time barricades, ancient barriers and obstructions. I destroy and violate every evil covenant, wicked counsel hanging over me and all your daughters, causing delays in conception in the name of Jesus. From today, all oaths from the pit of hell are broken in the name of Jesus. I decree that all ancient covenants, blood spells, negative curses, entered by myself or any of your daughters in error consciously or unconsciously, are destroyed in the mighty name of Jesus. Every evil spirit in my life is negated. Every Satanic demand on the destiny of Your children is hereby cancelled. I disentangle this marriage from satanic curses, spells, barriers, incense, divination, offerings, altars and I violate and overturn them in the mighty name of Jesus. Father, cause me and all your daughters to multiply according to Your Word. Dear Lord, increase us and cause us to be fruitful in the mighty name of Jesus.

Dear Father, once again, I decree that my wait is over in the mighty name of Jesus. At the resurrection, you declared it was finished and, on that anointing, I stand. I decree over my life and over other lives and say, it is finished in the mighty name of Jesus."

5. PRAYER OF PRAISE, ADORATION AND WORSHIP

This is simply a way of praising God by worshipping Him. We express our adoration for who He is, what He says and what He has done. Most of these praises can be found in the Scripture.

Say this prayer of praise and worship:

"My Father and my God, I praise you today. You are a faithful God who does no wrong. You're my fortress of salvation, a refuge for the needy in distress, an ever-present help in trouble. Eternal King! Defender of widows, God over the kingdoms of the earth. Great and awesome God. Great and powerful God. The I am who I am. The one who was, who is and who is to come. The Holy one of Israel. The one who made the heaven and earth. Mighty and everlasting God, immortal God, invisible God. The one who owns the cattle upon a thousand hills. The one who dwells in heaven. The one who dwells in light and yet no one can approach him. The mystery of all ages. The one whose hands form the deep places of the earth. The one who owns the strength of the hills. The one whose hands formed the dry land.

The Bible describes You in Psalm 104 as the one who is a very great God. The one who is clothed with honour and majesty. The one who covers himself with light as with a garment. The one who stretches out the heavens like a curtain. The one who lays the beams of His chambers in the waters: The one who makes the clouds his chariot, The one who walks upon the wings of the wind. The one who makes his angels spirits and His ministers a flaming fire.

The one who laid the foundations of the earth, that it should not be removed forever. The one who waters the hills from His chambers."

Unto you shall all flesh come. You're the bright and morning star. The lion of the tribe of Judah, the rod of Jesse. The root of David. The rose of Sharon. The lily of valley. The cedar in Lebanon.

Father, you're the one who calls those things that be not as though they were. The one who measures the length and breadth of the hills, mountains and sea. The one who kept and, preserved us from this evil world, I say, thank You.

I praise you, Judge of all the earth. King of glory.

Almighty God, You're the maker of all things. Maker of heaven and earth. My advocate, my comforter, my helper, my hiding place. My refuge and strength. The rock of my salvation. The rock in whom I take refuge. My dwelling place, my compass, my support, my song, and praise.

The only wise God. The compassionate and gracious God. The eternal God. The consuming fire. The glory of Israel. The spring of the living water. The strength of our heart.

Alpha and Omega. Ancient of Days. Author and finisher of our faith. Firstborn from among the dead. Great shepherd of the sheep. Bright and morning star.

Lord, You're Indescribable! Unattainable! Uncontainable! Unfathomable! Unsearchable! Unquestionable! Light of the world. You are the resurrection and the life. All powerful,

All knowing, All loving, Father, You're all sufficient God! Omnipotent! Omnipresent! And Omniscient!

The Bible says in Acts 17:28, *For in You we live and move and have our being.* In Jesus mighty name I have worshipped. Amen."

THE NUGGETS

A COLLECTION OF
THE SCRIPTURAL TRUTHS

NUGGET #1:

GUARD YOUR SALVATION

Some have argued that once a person is saved, the person never loses their salvation. That is not true. If you are saved, you must remain saved and continue to bear fruits until the trumpet sounds or you are called home by your maker.

I have been a strong beneficiary of the mercy of God through the prayer group at The Redeemed Christian Church of God (RCCG) for a while and my eyes have been opened to see beyond raising prayer points. In the few years that I have spent on earth, I have seen people rise and fall and even the mightiest organizations fall like giant dominoes crashing.

If you are reading this book, you're privileged to be reminded to watch your steps and treat the race with all the seriousness that it deserves. The Scripture in Philippians encourages us to work out our salvation in fear and trembling.

Dear friends, you always followed my instructions when I was with you. And now that I am away, it is even more important. Work hard to show the results of your salvation, obeying God with deep reverence and fear. For God is working in you, giving you the desire and the power to do what pleases him. (Philippians 2:12-13 NLT)

Salvation is not work you merit or something you must work for, rather, it is a gift from God that is given to you out of love by God's mercy and it is received by faith.

Working out your salvation is not the same as working for your salvation. In his letter to the church in Philippians, Apostle Paul encourages believers to work out their salvation and reminds them that this beautiful gift of salvation is inside of us, and its fruits must be made manifest in our lives. For a fledgling believer, this can bring trepidation at the beginning, but the Holy Spirit is there to help us live this out.

Apostle Paul in his letter to the Corinthians admonishes them to take heed so they would not stumble.

If you think you are standing strong, be careful not to fall. (1 Corinthians 10:12 NLT)

I started penning this book as a simple prayer for young and fledgling believers in Christ and I believe that is exactly what it will be able to accomplish. I have a burden to share a few of life's nuggets that I have learned over time, and I believe that anyone who reads them would find them helpful and beneficial. I believe I owe you a duty to encourage you to jealously guard the free salvation that you have received.

Regardless of your level of faith and maturity in Christ if you don't take heed as commanded in the Scriptures above, you will be left vulnerable.

If as a Christian you think you're too big to fall, then you must equally be too big to be a Christian.

No matter how much you have achieved in the Lord, no matter how far you have gone in your walk with Christ Jesus, no matter the amount or magnitude of miracles that God has wrought through you, you are vulnerable as soon as you step outside of Jesus. There is no guarantee that you will remain at the top if you let down your guard and there is no law of nature that even the most powerful will inevitably succeed and remain successful. Anyone can fall so, guard your salvation jealously.

Apostle Paul urged his spiritual son Timothy to run from evil.

"Run from anything that stimulates youthful lusts. Instead, pursue righteous living, faithfulness, love, and peace. Enjoy the companionship of those who call on the Lord with pure hearts." (2 Timothy 2:22 NLT)

Peter also forewarned us.

Stay alert! Watch out for your great enemy, the devil. He prowls around like a roaring lion, looking for someone to devour. Stand firm against him and be strong in your faith. Resist him, standing firm in the faith. (1 Peter 5:8-9a NLT)

No one is immune to temptations and tribulations of life so the best suggestion Scripture offers us is to steer clear of situations where we'll be tempted – positioning matters.

Temptation does not automatically equate sin. However, to invite temptation or yield to temptation is sinful. We must be careful not to let down our guard.

"A man who brings home ant-infested faggots should not be surprised when he is being visited by lizards." - African proverb

Positioning is important. We can invite temptation in different ways. We invite temptation when we use our imagination in sinful ways. We invite temptation to our lives when we deliberately go to places that make us vulnerable. Why are you going to the pub to evangelize if you are struggling with alcohol? Why visit a female member of your church alone when promiscuity is your problem? Why watch porn when your body chemistry doesn't respect the Holy Spirit? Why are you deliberately strolling near casino when you are struggling with gambling? Why are you letting someone draw you in to arguments on sports or politics when you are still struggling with anger and foul language and easily get provoked? Why carry a pack of cigarettes in your bag when you are trying to quit smoking?

We must be cautious and not give in to Satan.

And do not give the devil a foothold. (Ephesians 4:27 NIV)

Stay away from every kind of evil. (1 Thessalonians 5:22 NLT)

How close can you get to sin and still be a Christian? Ponder over it. The farther away you are from sin, the better it is for your spiritual life. Steer clear of sin!

There is a fable about an ambulance firm that was recruiting drivers and the test was centred on how close the driver could drive to a cliff but keep the ambulance from going over the edge. Many different applicants took the test. All the potential drivers who took the test shared their experiences on how close they drove to a cliff without toppling over the edge. One of them even said,

"I know I have got the job. I was so close to the cliff that the wheels were right over the edge of the cliff, and I drove right out without problems."

When the human resources representative finally came up to announce the candidate who passed the driving test, the job went to the driver who did not even drive anywhere near the cliff. The human resources staffer said,

"We want drivers who do not recklessly put our patients in unnecessary danger."

The moral of the story is that we should not let the choices we make harm our spiritual lives. Do not jeopardize your relationship with God by the decisions you make. Learn to resist the temptations that lurk around the corner.

A few years ago, I had flown to Miami in Florida through Washington DC as a doctoral student to see my academic supervisor. Jet-lagged, exhausted, and needed to lounge around, so I strolled outside the hotel where I had lodged in. Miami is so unique – a city that is overrun by fun – with most women walking the streets in their swimsuits. I walked to the front lounge through the foyer of the hotel, a young damsel approached me and without mincing words asked,

"You wanna have fun?" This was strange and scary. Where I came from, ladies don't usually make such brazen advances to men. She was beautiful and young, but I needed to flee. Somehow, I was able to spew out a few words, "Please give me your cellphone number and I will call in a few minutes. Wait here while I pick up something just across." I pretended to be in a hurry to pick up something at a nearby outlet.

She called out her number, I promised to call, and I left. I never called her. Instead, I hid and watched her from a corner and surreptitiously made my way back to my hotel room. That evening, I promised myself to be more vigilant.

Remove your way far from her, and do not go near the door of her house. (Proverbs 5:8 NKJV)

Temptation may not always be avoided so long as we live in this side of eternity, but we can be better prepared by deliberately living out the purpose of God in faith from His Word.

PRAYER POINTS:

1. My father and my God, there are many temptations to sin around me, please help me to always watch and pray so that I won't fall.
2. Father, please help me so that I am not at the wrong place at the wrong time or even at the right place at the wrong time. Help me to position my self always in Your Presence.
3. Father, do not allow me to fall into any temptation that will overcome me in the mighty name of Jesus.

A FISH OUT OF WATER?

People often boast in their accomplishments and material possessions, and this is because we identify them as giving us significance in life.

Go forward with a sense of purpose. There are more people who have failed through lack of purpose than lack of talent. You are wired to overcome circumstances, attain goals, solve problems and proffer solutions. You will never feel a sense of accomplishment, find real satisfaction or true happiness in life without overcoming obstacles except in a few cases where someone else close to you conquers them on your behalf.

Money does not bring true satisfaction. Often I hear people say they want more money when what they really need is satisfaction.

When Simeon saw that the Spirit was given at the laying on of the apostles' hands, he offered them money and said, "Give me also this ability so that everyone on whom I lay my hands may receive the Holy Spirit." Peter answered: "May your money perish with you, because you thought you could buy the gift of God with money!" (Acts 8:18-20 NIV)

I do not attempt to downplay the importance of money.

The Bible also says:

…but money answereth all things. (Ecclesiastes 10:19 KJV)

The point that I am making is we need to be driven by a true sense of purpose in seeking the will of God. We need to live a purpose driven life.

For everything in the world – the lust of the flesh, the lust of the eyes, and the pride of life – comes not from the Father but is from the world. The world and its desires pass away but whoever does the will of God lives forever. (1 John 2:16-17 NIV)

It's an effort in futility to dwell on worldly pleasures because they are transient and ephemeral.

I know there is much that money can buy such as cars, houses, clothes, etc. Money can even buy you a friend and could make someone eat humble pie. But money can never buy you true joy. It is important that Christians are content with what they have.

But godliness with contentment is great gain. For we brought nothing into this world, and we can take nothing out of it. (1 Timothy 6:6-7 NIV)

Better one handful with tranquility than two handfuls with toil and chasing after the wind. (Ecclesiastes 4:6 NIV)

While the lazy procrastinate until they are ruined, those who pursue wealth come to realize their efforts are meaningless and a miserable business. Don't confuse contentment with complacency. Once we confuse these two words, we end up having issues at our hands.

The desired balance is to relax from the toil of greedy grasping and find contentment in what truly belongs to us. For that which rightfully belongs to us always stays.

What good is it for someone to gain the whole world yet forfeit their soul. (Mark 8:36 NIV)

You need to ask the Lord's help to be content with what He has given you and to show genuine gratefulness always. Godliness with contentment is a great gain.

Money can not purchase the spiritual gifts of God and it is never a replacement for diligence and faithfulness to God's word. Money is good, but do not let the pursuit for it torpedo or ruin your relationship with your maker.

Seek the Kingdom of God above all else, and live righteously, and he will give you everything you need. (Matthew 6:33 NLT)

Let's consider seeking God's purpose in our lives through the lens of finding fulfillment.

What gives you a true sense of purpose? Do you sometimes feel like a fish out of water? What are the things that are driving you and what are you pursuing? Are you often dissatisfied in what you're doing? Dissatisfaction comes in many shades of gray. If there's prolonged dissatisfaction in your spirit and soul, then you were probably created for a different purpose other than what you are currently involved in.

For from Him and through Him and for Him are all things... (Romans 11:36 NIV)

For in Him we live, and move and have our being ... (Acts 17:28 KJV)

God is everything to you and without Him, you are nothing. This is exactly what it means to be like fish in the water. All that a fish knows is water. Their entire life is water and water only. When you grab fish and pull them out of water onto a patch of dry soil - different habitat - where there's no water, the fish begin to struggle for their life. The moment the fish are placed on that dry land, they become unpleasant and motionless, The fish will gasp for oxygen, flop around helplessly and begin to die.

And just before it dies, if you are fast enough to carefully place the fish back in the stream, the dying fish suddenly make some splashes for a few seconds and begin to swim away effortlessly. Fish thrive in their true habitat. This is like a liquid ballet. What ease and what beauty!

No matter how long the fish lay there on the dry soil, even if they didn't die, they would never adapt. The fish would never adjust and survive the new environment and would only struggle. And it would never be satisfied with the new habitat no matter how hard you tried to force it. Even if the fish convinced themselves that they could learn to like the patch of dry soil, they would never thrive. If these fish remained on the dry soil, death was inevitable for them.

Do you feel like a fish out of water? Are you experiencing a prolonged dissatisfaction in your course of study or you are not content with your current job? Give heed to these signals because they could be pointing to the fact that you were created for another purpose. And like those fish, if you feel like you are dying inside, then pay attention. It could be just what you need to push you into another, more satisfying life.

... for without Me you can do nothing. (John 15:5 NKJV)

You can't be all that God has created you to be without Him inside of you. Never!

Everyone knows that water is the habitat of fish. Water was made for fish and fish were made for water. Water is their life, and they simply can't survive without it. This is exactly how it is for every born-again child of God. Jesus Christ is the believer's habitat and that is where they live. For without Him, we can do nothing. Without Him, we are like fish out of water.

Check your pulse. Do you easily get fired up about the despicable state of things around you? Do you get comfortable or hurt whenever you hear about the cruelty meted out to little children or animals? Are you easily moved by people's desperate conditions or does a story of someone else's heartbreak grieve your heart? Does talking about Jesus Christ stir up your passion? Then listen to these signals. In addition to your God-given talents or gift, they could possibly be pointing to where your purpose lies. You need to find your God-given purpose in life.

Several passages of the Scripture confirm the fact that every one of us was created by God and born into this world to fulfill God's purpose.

For by him were all things created, that are in heaven, and that are in earth, visible and invisible, whether they be thrones, or dominions, or principalities, or powers: all things were created by him, and for him. (Colossians 1:16 KJV)

There's nothing like an afterthought with God. Everything He does is purposeful and deliberate. Not only that, He has everything to the minutest detail, precisely tied to time.

To every thing there is a season, and a time to every purpose under the heaven. (Ecclesiastes 3:1 KJV)

When you study the Bible, you will observe that from Adam and Eve, to Noah, Abraham, Joseph, Moses, Saul, David, and all the prophets and kings, they all were precisely designed according to God's ultimate plan. All things that have ever happened on earth and in heaven were ordered according to His unsearchable wisdom.

Known unto God are all his works from the beginning of the world. (Acts 15:18 KJV)

John the Baptist fulfilled his purpose by preparing the way for the Lord and announcing the arrival of Jesus, baptizing Him, confronting the sinfulness and rebellion of that generation and preaching the repentance of sins. Jeremiah's purpose as a prophet of God was clearly described to root out, pull down, to destroy and throw down, to build and to plan in Jeremiah 1:1-10. These two prophets were able to fulfill God's purpose.

Seeking fulfillment in life is almost universal. However, the primary problem stems from the fact that while everyone knows when they were born, only few know why they were born. That's why they are searching for meaning.

If I asked at church gathering by show of hands how many people believe that God has a purpose for their lives, almost every hand would be raised. Yet if I asked how many people know why they were born or their God-given purpose, only a few hands would remain in the air. What does this mean?

Most people are living life without knowing what their purpose is. Nonetheless, they yearn to live meaningful lives. One of Satan's most convincing lies is to tell you that God does not have a purpose for you or that you cannot possibly know your purpose. Satan whispers things like:

"You are in this world by chance" or "Your existence is random." or "God doesn't even know that you exist."

These are all lies. Never listen to Satan.

Nothing is by accident with God, and nothing takes Him by surprise. God is faithful, but you must remember His timing is perfect. He's never a slave to your calendar. God is never too late or too early on anything. Wait on His timing.

If it ever seems like your life is missing something or like your life lacks significance, it's probably because you do not know what your purpose is. Jesus' purpose was to preach. This was also the purpose of the early apostles. Finding our purpose involves two basic questions. The first is identity: "Who am I?" The second is impact: "What is my purpose in life?"

Every one of us has a unique God-given purpose which only you can fulfill. Each of you should seek to discover exactly what that purpose is and live it out. God's purpose for your life is far greater than your own personal ideas, greater than your peace of mind or even your happiness. Life will not be complete until you discover your purpose. It will last longer than your career, your family, your ministry, or even your ambitions and dreams. To know why you were born in this world, you must begin with God. You were born by His purpose and for His purpose alone.

In seeking their purpose, many guess, theorize, predict, or postulate. How do you discover what you were created for? You basically have two options: by speculation or through revelation.

Ask the Holy Spirit for wisdom. If you want to find your purpose, look to revelation through prayer, dreams, visions, or even through daily whispers or the small still voice.

When you find God, destiny will find you. If there's no relationship, you will not come to know your purpose. Don't spend time doing things that rob you of time in God's presence. When you encounter God, He will cause your fire to burn as it did for Moses at the burning bush. There's nothing more powerful in life than living out the purpose that God has ordained just for you. It is when you are doing that – that is when you will feel most truly alive.

PRAYER POINTS:

1. Father, from today, I desire earnestly in my heart to have a strong personal relationship with you through Jesus.
2. Father, please reveal to me the purpose for which you have placed me here on earth in the mighty name of Jesus. Daddy, help me to fulfill my destiny according to your purpose for me in this part of eternity in the mighty name of Jesus.
3. Daddy, I know the proof of passion is pursuit. Father, please help me to develop passion for your spiritual gifts and work.

KNOW YOUR WORTH
IN CHRIST JESUS

In a seminar, a speaker held up a $100 bill while over a hundred people were listening to him.

"Who would like this hundred-dollar bill?" asked the speaker.

Almost everyone raised their hands in the air.

"I am going to give one hundred dollars to one of you, but first let me do this," he said and crumpled the $100 bill.

"Who still wants the money?" he asked.

All the hands remained in the air.

"What if I do this?" he said, throwing the $100 bill on the floor and grinding it with the sole of his shoe. The $100 bill was visibly crumpled and dirty and he asked again, "Now who wants it?"

Still all hands went into the air again.

"My friends, you have all learned a very valuable lesson. Even with all the crumpling and marching of the bill by my shoe, you still desired to have the money," he said. "Why? Because it did not devalue in its worth. The value of the $100 bill is still the same."

Many of us often put our self worth in the type of car we drive, the house we own and live in, the clothes we wear, and the things we don on our bodies. Some look to their financial status, stocks invested or number of companies they own. Others seek to their accomplishments, academic certificates, and their relationships. This can lead to you being broken and depressed. As important as these seem in the world, the Bible calls them vanity.

On the contrary, self-image based on the value God Himself has placed on us is Jesus-centred and goes far beyond our mortal imagination. As true believer, you must live as someone valued by God whose worth is in Christ.

Why are you valuable to God? You're valuable because of who you are. You are created in God's image and according to His likeness. You are God's vestige.

And God said, let us make man in our image, after our likeness: and let them have dominion over the fish of the sea, and over the fowl of the air, and over the cattle, and over all the earth, and over every creeping thing that creepeth upon the earth. (Genesis 1:26 KJV)

Remember your worth or value is based on what you cost. Your adoption into the lineage of Christ Jesus came at a high cost.

Having predestinated us unto the adoption of children by Jesus Christ to himself, according to the good pleasure of his will. To the praise of the glory of his grace, wherein he hath made us accepted in the beloved. In whom we have redemption through his blood, the forgiveness of sins, according to the riches of his grace. (Ephesians 1:5-7 KJV)

You are also valuable because Satan knows your potential and what you can become in the kingdom agenda.

In him we have obtained an inheritance, having been predestined according to the purpose of him who works all things according to the counsel of his will. So that we who were first to hope in Christ might be to the praise of his glory. (Ephesians 1:11-12 ESV)

It is important to know that your worth in Christ Jesus depends on your value. The value God has placed on you is the same value you should place on yourself. You can only live as someone with value if you know you are valued by God and this can only happen when you know the truth.

Remember that how you feel will naturally impact the way you live your life and how you relate with others. If you are a teenager or youth, you need to grasp and appreciate your worth because if you don't, people won't treat you with the respect and dignity that you deserve. This may mean that people will talk to you negatively, tend to abuse you in relationships or even look for every opportunity to be critical of you. It is only when young people do not know their true worth that they can remain in a hurtful relationship because they think they cannot find better relationship other than the one they are in.

But we have this treasure in earthen vessels, that the excellency of the power may be of God, and not of us. (2 Corinthians 4:7 KJV)

We take our money to the bank for safe keeping because we value money. So, where you take your body to or who you submit your body to speaks volumes about what you value. As a young girl, if you value your body as God values you, then you won't submit that precious body of yours to any man before marriage. The only reason a young person would submit their body to anyone before marriage is because they don't know their worth. The same applies to any married man or woman who is frolicking with someone else who isn't their spouse.

Stop spending too much time to beautify your outside appearance – be modest because your true worth lies on the inside. You want to decide on life partner or who to marry? Focus on the person's insides and don't let the wrapping fool you. Don't look at the face value. Real or true worth is found inside.

The more we know God's love for us, the more we love ourselves. The central message about the whole essence of Christ's death on the cross is that God values us enough to send His only begotten Son on our behalf.

For God so loved the world that he gave his one and only Son, that whoever believes in him shall not perish but have eternal life. (John 3:16 NIV)

His gift of grace is dependent upon our worth to Him and our value in Christ Jesus. Have you been hurt in the past because of someone taking advantage of you and not valuing you enough? Have you been battered in a relationship with others or you are feeling so hurt that you almost hate yourself? Are you plagued with shame and reproach by what has happened to you in the past or based on the reproach you have had to pass through?

God longs for you to truly believe that you are His treasure. If you're ready to accept Him, He is also ready to use you regardless of how much you think you have messed up. God is ready to empower you amid all your struggle. God wants to bring out your real value right where you are and make you into what He wants you to be. And it is only when you recognize that as a child of God that you are inherently special to Him, that you will be open and ready to experience His love and mercy. Start off by loving yourself first.

You shall love your neighbour as yourself. (Mark 12:31)

The Bible explains that by loving yourself first, only then you can love others. If you don't love yourself, you simply just won't be able to love your neighbours. Start by focusing on the extent of God's love to you. Accept God's love and come to the realization that you are so special to God. This involves learning how to forgive yourself for past mistakes, being kind to yourself and persevering as you go through rough times while remaining hopeful for a bright future.

For I know the plans I have for you, declares the Lord, plans to prosper you and not to harm you, plans to give you hope and a future. (Jeremiah 29:11 NIV)

God has a special plan for you, so do not let anything of the world take away your true worth.

Nothing outside Jesus can give you value or make you feel valuable. God calls you a masterpiece. You are one of a kind. You didn't just drop off from an assembly line during production in error. You weren't mass produced. God made you so special.

You're unique in God's creation and there will never be another you. Have you made some mistakes in the past? Have you been hurt in an unhealthy relationship in the past? Start carrying yourself with confidence because you have been fearfully and wonderfully made. Don't let anyone or situation define who you are or your worth.

God is saying to you right now: "You are amazing. You're good just the way you are. Come let's begin on a new slate."

Even if everyone abandons you, God will never abandon you. People may leave you out during discussions and may not seek your contributions, but God never leaves you out.

If David needed his family's approval to become a king, he would have never taken the throne. Don't give you up on yourself.

Look deeper, beneath the colours and contours of your life. If you have truly turned from your old ways, then your life has a new meaning.

People in the world understand how this works and tend to cash in on it. Just weeks before publishing this book, I remember the story of Michaela Coel.

In 2017, Michaela Coel turned down a million-dollar deal with Netflix for her show entitled, I May Destroy You.

Why on earth would someone, an ordinary immigrant you might say, turn down such an offer? It was because Netflix would not allow her to maintain any percentage of the copyright. Not even a single percentage point. So, she walked away from both Netflix and her agency, that was pushing her to take the deal.

A few months later, Michaela pitched the show to BBC and they gave her everything she desired in a contract including a seat at the development table and full creative control. HBO joined as a co-producer, while Michaela wrote all the twelve episodes, co-directed nine out of them and starred in the show.

On September 19, 2021, Michaela Coel made history at 2021 Emmys, becoming the first black woman to win the award for Outstanding Writing for a Limited Anthology Series and Movie for I May Destroy You. Fans all over the world celebrated Coel's history making win and her first ever Emmy.

We can see that even in secular things, people who know their worth tend to optimize the value they place on themselves not to mention those who are believers whose worth is in Christ Jesus. The world cannot take away your worth if your worth does not come from the world.

Let your worth come from being in the perfect will of God. Your greatest fulfillment will not come from your fat bank account or your earthly possessions, but by knowing that you serve the purpose of God here on earth.

PRAYER POINTS:

1. Father, help me to know my worth in you and to seek things of eternal value. Father, help me as Your child to see the good things that you have in store for me in the mighty name of Jesus.
2. Father, by your mercy, let me lay hold of my true worth in You and help me to know and exercise the authority You have granted me as a believer in the mighty name of Jesus.
3. Lord, please give me another opportunity to start with a clean slate and use me as your vessel in the mighty name of Jesus.

ABSOLUTE DEPENDENCE ON GOD

Growing up, as early as age 11, I started managing my personal funds and possessed more money than many adults around my life. When I was about 17, I owned my own motorcycle and had sufficient funds to purchase a plot of land, which I almost did. Since then, I worked hard (not sure I was working smart) and I gained everything I needed. I paid my school and tuition fees almost my entire life (from secondary school through to graduate and post-graduate degrees) including the tuition fees of my siblings. While as a student, I made my first million (in Naira) and owned two supermarkets, a hair salon as well as a business centre all within the campus of the University of Jos. I was very industrious and lacked nothing.

Students from wealthy homes, whose parents worked in the upper echelons of government, would borrow money from me. I don't recall ever borrowing money from anyone. I was awarded the most industrious and popular student at the time in department at the university and I was supporting my parents even as a teenager. In fact, I single-handedly raised nearly £18,000 (Pound Sterling) to fund my tuition fees for my master's degree at a university in Great Britain.

I thought that was all life could give, but I was dead wrong. I didn't realize that it was God who had helped me. I thought money answers all things, but I was so wrong! I never knew that I was enjoying God's mercy until He allowed me to pass through certain experiences that altered my viewpoint.

I was wrong in my mindset and perspective. I was a go it alone person who thought success came from simply working hard without Jesus at the centre of it. During this period, I believed all I needed to do was work hard, make good grades and pursue money.

Deep inside of me, I never depended on or looked at God as my supplier because I was doing well. Yes, I was religious, I was going to church on the outside, but my spirit was far from God.

I did not realize what the Scripture says:

And you shall remember the Lord your God, for it is He who gives you power to get wealth…. (Deuteronomy 8:18 NKJV)

Then some things happened in my life that literally changed my belief system. I ran into troubles that money could not solve. My father became ill and bedridden in the hospital. Given that no one else in my family was financially stable, it was up to me to pay for his hospital bills and medications. We had a family schedule where everyone would take turns to spend the night in the hospital with him. . Not all my siblings were in the same city as I was at the time, so we had limited human resources.

Other families found a way to manage their loved ones when they were hospitalized, but I had just started a new job in a bank. When it was my turn to spend the night at the hospital, I had to drive to the hospital after work and return to the office the next morning without a shower or rest.

Life was becoming difficult, especially when the routine had no end in sight. On multiple occasions, I would make vows to God and say to Him that I would give a specified amount of money in return for getting me out of those troubles. I was financially stable, but money was no longer a solution. I suffered, I prayed with tears and learned very important lessons of my life. My orientation changed.

Daily dependence on God is the only thing He wants from us.

These things I have spoken to you, that in Me you may have peace. In the world, you will have tribulation; but be of good cheer; I have overcome the world. (John 16:33 NKJV)

I was selective in the times I would trust God. Apparently, I suffered from the disease of compartmentalization, whereby I merely make God one component of my life and put other aspects of my life in another compartment. I thought I needed to trust God and pray earnestly only when I had no money or when things were rough. But this is not the sort of life that God calls us into. Only in Christ can one find real peace and victory to overcome obstacles of this life.

I still face situations where money is not the solution. In fact, recently I told my wife that I was going to send a good sum of money to her to travel. I was surprised at how quickly she shut down that idea out of my head. This was because we – my wife, the children and I - have been separated for long and it's been nearly two years since we came together as a family. The last time we met was during our last trip to London and Liverpool in December 2019.

Today, I have learned that one of the reasons why God allows such troubles and trials in my life is because it is His way of teaching me to depend on him daily. God wants to be the first option in my life and not the last resort. In hindsight, I should have trusted Him completely from the outset.

God wants us to have total dependence on Him through faith and not on our own strength.

He will keep the feet of his saints, and the wicked shall be silent in darkness; for by strength shall no man prevail. (1 Samuel 2:9 KJV)

God is present everywhere and He alone rules all things. From the microcosm to the macrocosm, He's in charge. This is the more reason why we must depend solely on Him. The Scriptural account of the creation of man by God provides us with the utter dependence of the created man on the creator,

God. Any other cynical attempt to grasp the concept of humans and their proper place in the created universe will often result in depravity and utter confusion.

Faith in God is like deciding to jump out of a plane and expecting God to catch you. And if God does not catch or guide every of your step, you will fall and crash. This is the kind of dependence that God is looking for in us.

PRAYER POINTS:

1. Father, please teach me to depend on You every day of my life.
2. I want to depend on You, Lord when the going is good and when the going is bad in the mighty name of Jesus.
3. Father, I want to learn to have complete faith in You. Holy Spirit, please help me.

NUGGET #5

INVEST IN OTHERS:
Scatter Your Sunlight

Cast thy bread upon the waters: for thou shall find it after many days. (Ecclesiastes 11:1 KJV)

One of my powerful motivations in life growing up as a young boy who was the first child in a family of seven then, was to help my siblings and the people around me succeed. This principle has been intrinsic and has fuelled many of my life's decisions. While I was growing up, I understood the principle that elevates community or collective empowerment rather than individualism. So, I made up my mind early in life to help not only my family, but as many people as I can. There is no investment you can make in your lifetime that can pay you so much as the effort to scatter sunshine and good cheer into other people's lives.

The Christian faith encourages us to help others and the Bible says:

Therefore, as we have opportunity, let us do good to all people, especially to those who belong to the family of believers. (Galatians 6:10 NIV)

Those who are wise will shine as bright as the sky, and those who lead many to righteousness will shine like the stars forever. (Daniel 12:3 NLT)

"You can have everything in life you want, if you will just help enough other people get what they want." - Zig Ziglar

By the grace of God and with a deep sense of humility, from time to time, I receive feedback and greetings from a few old classmates who I helped even in little things such as helping to solve academic assignments and workloads in class. And others that I cannot mention here so that I don't lose my reward. It always refreshes my soul.

Your contribution can have a lifelong impact on others. Give up fame, give up worldly popularity and serve humanity. Understand that greatness is not deposited in you to stay, but rather to flow to others through you.

Remember that you cannot hold a light to another person's path without brightening your own path. Invest in others and the dividends will outlive you.

By the grace of God, five of my siblings graduated (lost one at her final year though) from public universities and one from a private university. In all sense of humility and to the glory of God, I singlehandedly bankrolled their tuitions, books and living expenses. It wasn't an obligation, but it was the right thing to do. I am currently doing the same for two of my nieces as well.

Love people more than you think they deserve and don't miss a chance of helping others. In fact, as little as this may seem, never lose a chance of saying a kind word to people you meet. Humans matter so much to God therefore, for those of us who seek to reflect God's glory in our lives, we must value people including valuing the unborn babies. Think of simple things you can do from time to time to reflect godliness in our behaviour and relationship with others.

"You will find as you look back upon your life that the moments when you have really lived, are the moments when you have done things in the spirit of love." – Henry Drummond

There's always a beneficial reward for good deeds meted out with a right motive. The Bible tells us:

Do not be deceived, God is not mocked; for whatever a man sows, that he will also reap. (Galatians 6:7 NKJV)

Viewing it through the lens of a farmer, there are three things that are given when it comes to sowing and reaping:

1. You reap what you sow
2. You reap more than what you sow
3. You reap later than when you sow

I know it can be hard to consider other's needs while we're still anxious about ours, but we are called to be different.

Therefore, as we have opportunity, let us do good to all people. Make every effort to sow seeds of kindness, encouragement, love, forgiveness and help one another in the faith. As little as finding time to listen to people and being present when they truly need your presence can make a huge difference. That way we can harvest the fruits that come along with it and by so doing, we can lay up for ourselves treasures in heaven.

In his book, The Success Journey, John Maxwell defines success as

"knowing your purpose in life, growing to reach your maximum potential and sowing seeds to benefit others. No matter how long you live or what you decide to do in life, you will never exhaust your capacity to grow toward your potential or run out of opportunities to help others."

Through helping others, we find and fulfill our God-given purpose in life. There are many professions that focus on meeting other people's needs. Doctors, nurses, paramedics, police and firefighters all help to save lives. There is always a beneficial reward on any act of kindness done with a right motive. The Scripture says:

Do not be deceived, God is not mocked; for whatever a man sows, that he will also reap. For he who sows to his flesh will of the flesh reap corruption, but he who sows to the Spirit will of the Spirit reap everlasting life. (Galatians 6:7-8 NKJV)

I mean that I want us to help each other with faith we have. Your faith will help me, and my faith will help you. (Romans 1:12 NCV)

Share each other's troubles and problems, and in this way obey the law of Christ. If you think you are too important to help someone in need, you are only fooling yourself. You are really a nobody. Be sure to do what you should, for then you will enjoy the personal satisfaction of having done your work well, and you won't need to compare yourself to anyone else. (Galatians 6:2-4 NLT).

Read and ruminate on this folk tale about a king who had twin boys. There had been some confusion about which of these sons was the first born. The king was getting older and the boys were becoming men gradually with time. As they grew, the king was desperately seeking a fair way to designate one of them as crown prince to succeed him.

One fateful day, he invited them to join him in his council chamber for a talk.

"My sons, the day will come when one of you must succeed me as a king. The task of the kingdom is so enormous, and burdens of sovereignty are very heavy. To find out which of you is better able to bear them cheerfully, I am sending you together to a far corner of the kingdom. One of my advisors there will place equal loads on your shoulders. My crown will one day go to the one who first returns bearing his burden just exactly as a king should."

In the spirit of fairness, the twin brothers embarked on the journey together. Not long after the journey began, they came upon a frail old woman who was struggling under a heavy load. One of the boys said, "We have a burden of our own to worry about. Let us be on our way." But the other boy suggested that they stop to help the aged woman.

The first brother hurriedly left, while the second one helped the woman.

On his trip to the kingdom's edge, the same young man found other people in desperate need of aid. He helped a lost child reunite with his anxious parents. He found a blind woman who needed help to get back home. He also met a farmer whose wagon required a strong shoulder to push it out of the mud.

When finally, he arrived at the destination, he met with father's advisor, secured his load and started his journey back home. When he returned to the palace, his brother who had reached there before him welcomed him at the entrance.

"I don't understand," he said with dismay. "I told father the burden was too heavy to carry. How did you manage it alone?"

His brother, who apparently won the competition, responded.

"I suppose when I helped others carry their burdens, I found the strength to carry my own."

Bear each other's burden and in this way, you will be obeying the law of Christ. As Christians, we are all called to help people in carrying their loads.

I know everyone is busy running after money to pay their bills, but there's nothing stopping you from pausing to help someone.

Without being intrusive, make the effort to find out what is going on in their life. Don't just pass or walk on by.

"How can I help you? How can I be of help? How is it going with you and your household? Are you okay?"

We should not be self-centred, thinking only of our own needs. Try to deliberately take your mind off your own troubles for a moment, then open your eyes and look at the struggles in the lives of the people around you. It's not always easy, but you might be surprised what you discover, You're likely not the only one dealing with issues.

When we start helping others grow by carrying their burdens, inexplicable joy and strength comes to our inner lives, along with a sense of satisfaction and fulfillment.

The ongoing COVID-19 pandemic ravaging us shows that the world is indeed a global village. The virus exposed how connected humans are to each other and how we all depend on one another. Take the mask mandate. We are told that wearing a mask protects others more than it does to the person wearing it.

It also raises some pertinent questions to ask ourselves. What would it be like to judge my well-being in terms of the well-being of others? How much is my happiness tied to the common good of the society? What would it mean to think more in terms of our shared vulnerability as a people, rather than securing our own individual well being?

Build your community. Ask your friends to join you in a community-building activity. You could use your business place to mentor a group of local youths for example. Open your eyes to see the needs of your local community and make effort to make positive impact. Share your skills and mentor young entrepreneurs or throw your weight behind a good cause. You never know, a better world could begin in that workplace. It is your choice.

From the first day Jason Benham opened a sporting goods store in his own neighbourhood, he made up his mind to become more than just another shopkeeper. When he discovered that the store's clientele was mostly neighbourhood teenagers and young adults, many of whom faced challenges such as peer pressure, depression, poverty and opioid related violence, Benham felt he could relate with them.

Benham put up a basketball hoop outside his store where local youths could play in a safe environment. From that moment, Benham Sports morphed into a gathering place for the community's youths. Benham created a space where they could seek counsel and find inspiration, a spot to study as well as shoot hoops. As he watched these young teenagers and youths grew up, he observed an intriguing trend. The young teenagers who hung out at his store were not getting into trouble anymore but the ones who stayed away from his store did. Parents of these youths noticed the same thing and stopped by to meet him. They thanked him, not only for giving their children a spot to hang out, but also for helping the boys with their resumes, providing them with references guiding them through their homework and even tutoring them during their exams.

Benham's wife later told some people that her husband measures his success on a different scale. He considers the smiles on their faces, the confidence in their step, their grades in school as well as the jobs they have been able to get because of his support. Through his efforts, young people who might otherwise have turned to less socially responsible activities have found a sense of purpose and belonging. Even though Benham's positive work was informal, it is a thriving part of this community and a flourishing enterprise with a big heart.

Care for others. Even in modern organizations, having a caring manager is increasingly becoming a prerequisite for successful management and this has profoundly shaped the evolving management theory in the twenty-first century. This trait underpins most great leaders across all spheres of life. Suffice it to say that leaders who are perceived as not to care about their followers will not be able to completely engage them, and without this engagement, optimal performance will remain a mirage.

Character is like clothing that we wear and if you have a godly character, it is like putting the Jesus label on display.

Therefore, as God's chosen people, holy and dearly loved, clothe yourselves with compassion, kindness, humility, gentleness, and patience. Bear with each other and …And over all these virtues put on love, which bind them together in perfect unity. (Colossians 3:12-14 NIV)

These are not meant to be our "Sunday clothes" or "workplace clothes", we're to wear them everywhere to reflect Christ in our lives.

Kindness is an attribute of God. Show God's love through act of kindness. This is called, servant evangelism. Open your eyes to understand the power of kindness in evangelism – bearing fruits that will abide. Be wise in the manner you act toward people; make the most of every opportunity to win unbelievers to Christ. This is the Great Commission! (Matthew 28:18-20)

Let your conversation be gracious and attractive so that you will have the right response for everyone. (Colossians 4:6 NLT)

When we show act of kindness and the love of Christ to others, they may very well see the need to be saved.

Sometimes, our success is measured by the impact we make and the joy we bring to others and our communities. The future is often created by what we do today and even small movements can bring about huge changes. When you lift one another up and empower communities it can last more than a lifetime. Let us do our best to leave the world a better place than we found it. What connects us is thinking of we instead of me.

PRAYER POINTS:

1. Father, help me to cast my bread upon water and scatter sunlight that I may live to glorify you
2. Lord, use me to bless generation and let me be a blessing to others in the mighty name of Jesus.
3. Dear Lord, open my eyes to see other's needs and bless me so that I in turn can bless them in the mighty name of Jesus.

LITTLE THINGS ARE SPRINGBOARDS

Be faithful in little things. Several accounts in the Scripture offer us a glimpse of how God has accomplished great things from seemingly little things or things that started out so small that short-sighted people looked down on them.

Scripture describes one account in Ezra 4:4-11 where what started out as little thing became a huge project. It tells us that after the emancipation from the Babylonian exile, God used a king named Cyrus to lead His remaining children back to Jerusalem and Judah. Zerubbabel returned with a team of Jewish expatriates who rebuilt the temple which had been destroyed by the Babylonians. People mocked them and looked at the project with derision.

*The people of the land tried to discourage the people of Judah.
They troubled them in building and hired counselors against them
to frustrate their purpose all the days of Cyrus king of Persia, even
until the reign of Darius king of Persia. (Ezra 4:4-5 NKJV)*

Consequently, many of these Jews made mockery of God's
project and balked at those deliberate efforts and even
despised the days of little beginnings. Most of these Jews
failed to grasp the truth: there are no little things with God.
At least we can relate with the account of two fish and five
loaves of bread in the gospel of Matthew.

Let us not digress from the main story. The Bible tells us the
angel of the Lord appeared unto Zerubbabel and encouraged
him to complete the work he had been called to do.

Although it may appear impossible at the beginning, there
is always light at the end of the tunnel when God is in the
centre of it.

*With men this is impossible, but with God all things are possible.
(Matthew 19:26 KJV)*

*Who are you, O great Mountain? Before Zerubbabel you shall
become a plain. (Zechariah 4:7 ESV)*

"Trowel and hammer, saw and plane are instruments of
vanity unless the Lord be the Master builder." - Charles
Spurgeon

God encouraged Zerubbabel and assured him of the needed
grace to finish the work.

The hands of Zerubbabel have laid the foundation of this temple; his hands will also complete it. Then you will know that the Lord Almighty has sent me to you. (Zechariah 4:9 NIV)

Does the path you're travelling capture your motivation? A belief isn't just an idea a person possesses, it is an idea that possesses a person. A value isn't just what a person holds so dear, it is that something that holds a person. Find something that consumes you and recreate it.

Work willingly at whatever you do, as though you were working for the Lord rather than for people. Remember that the Lord will give you inheritance as your reward, and that the Master you are serving is Christ. (Colossians 3:23-24 NLT)

Stay motivated in the course you believe in and learn to be comfortable with being enthusiastic. No force is as powerful as motivation. There are opportunities in life that come to you as springboard to something bigger ahead and it requires your all. Give it all your heart, spirit, soul, and time. Do not underestimate the potential inherent in any opportunity no matter how small it appears.

When you are faithful in those little things that have been committed to you to manage, only then can you prove yourself ready for more.

The master was full of praise. "Well done, my good and faithful servant. You have been faithful in handling this small amount, so now I will give you many more responsibilities. Let's celebrate together!" (Matthew 25:21 NLT)

Do you want your pastor to entrust you with a bigger responsibility? Do you desire to be promoted in your job? Do you desire that your father give you higher authority or powers in his business? Do you want God to give you bigger testimonies? Then you must be accountable for the seemingly small stuff already committed in your care. Achieving excellence in anything requires strong motivation and passion.

Never think that you are too big for any task. Small opportunities are often the beginning of great investment and enterprises.

Life is a journey, not a destination and the small steps we take today will eventually shape our path for better tomorrow. The ideal way to better your lot is to strive for more and build on the lot you have been given in life. The starting point of every accomplishment is desire. Motivation is the key to any accomplishment.

"A strong passion for any object will ensure success, for the desire of the end will point out the means." -William Hazlitt

According to Lewis B. Smedes, passion involves three things: motivation, belief, and investment.

I heard a story about a young girl that was sent to bed by her mother.

A few minutes later, she screamed, "Mom!"

"What is it?" asked her mom.

"Mommy, I'm thirsty. Please can I have a cup of water?"

"I told you no. You had your chance to drink it earlier and if you ask again, I will have to spank you."

Four minutes later, the little girl called out yet again.

"What?" replied her mom.

"When you come in to spank me, can you bring a cup of water for me, please?"

If you were that mom, what would you do? The motivation to achieve your result or see a desired outcome was at play here.

Ideas can be like rabbits. You learn some tricks and how to apply them and before you know it, there are more. Learn to always frustrate convention and traditions with your creativity and imagination. Let your imagination roam and give it oxygen. Don't forget that opportunities are only limited by your imagination and when you are motivated, your imagination can roam unimpeded.

I believe Jesus wouldn't be impressed when you shirk your responsibilities, but He might respect your ingenuity. How did I know? In Luke 16, Jesus told us a strange story about a business manager whose job was terminated and on his final day in the office, he did something astonishing. This manager slashed the bills of his master's debtors.

I tell you, use worldly wealth to gain friends for yourselves, so that when it is gone, you will be welcomed into eternal dwellings. (Luke 16:9 NIV)

We know that Jesus didn't praise the manager's deception instead, Jesus applauded the man's creativity and shrewdness and wished that believers would be clever as well.

God is omniscient and humans are intelligent because God created them in His own image. Though, your intelligence is just an inkling of His, you have been greatly endowed to create literally anything as far as your mind can conceive.

Find passion to match your motivation. Your growth must be consistent with your value. Do not confuse growth with excellence because growth does not equal excellence and big does not equal great.

You don't have to do something totally out of the blue to be great and you don't need to pursue a blockbuster to be relevant. Let your growth be built upon noble purposes far beyond fame and money. Let the culture of purpose and excellence thrive and do not allow mediocrity to creep in.

Never give up on the principles that define who you are in Christ Jesus. Be ready to sever ties with distractors and even friends who do not add value to your Kingdom pursuits.

Be willing to evolve and embrace the inevitability of destruction, but never give up on creating and living your dream according to God's will. I have always envisioned my books on the shelves of the world best libraries and by God's grace, that will happen.

Do not forget that the path of darkness often starts with those exasperatingly persistent people who are incapable of capitulation. I am not encouraging you to take risks that could blow holes below the waterlines, but to stay focused and faithful even in little things which have been placed in your care.

PRAYER POINTS:

1. Father, open my eyes to opportunities and help me to see things that others can't see
2. Father, create a path for me that no man can follow and launch me to stardom in the mighty name of Jesus.
3. Father, give me the passion and motivation to excel in every little task or assignment that has been given to me in the mighty name of Jesus.

NUGGET #7

SACRIFICE TO GROW: NO PAIN NO GAIN

Therefore, I urge you, brothers, and sisters, in view of God's mercy, to offer your bodies as a living sacrifice, holy and pleasing to God—this is your true and proper worship. (Romans 12:1 NIV)

I'm confused when I see Christians attempt to introduce efficiency and effectiveness in their walk with God, making it look like everything can be painless and quick. It doesn't work that way. We must be reminded that Christianity is not about finding a cheaper and better way to serve God. It is a call to sacrifice. It is a call to a higher duty. One of the toughest times to be a Christian is to obey God when it does not seem like there is a practical reason to do so.

Sacrifice involves letting go of what we cherish. It is a personal choice and sometimes the choice to sacrifice or not is entirely ours to make.

The life of Jesus epitomizes sacrifice of servanthood, which culminated in His horrific death to liberate mankind from eternal damnation.

The first step to sacrifice involves surrender. This simply means to relinquish all your possessions to another person, or to submit to the authority of someone else. To sacrifice means to give up something and it is usually at great expense to ourselves.

If anyone desires to come after Me, let him deny himself, and take up his cross daily and follow Me. (Luke 9:23 NKJV)

Who gave Himself for us, that He might redeem us from every lawless deed and purify for Himself His own special people, zealous for good works. (Titus 2:14 NKJV)

Make a list of some of the things you value such as money, loved ones, time, peace, comfort, sleep, etc. Take a closer look at your list and you may be shocked that some of the plans or approaches to achieve them often conflict with God's own plan. Yes, God's blessings include all these things, but our surrender to God's purpose should be a statement that we are not living our lives for these things because they are not an end but just a means. Jesus does not just look at the substance being sacrificed; He looks at the heart.

Jesus Christ also warns that pain and suffering would be a part of our lives when we obey to make sacrifices.

I have told you all this so that you may have peace in me. Here on earth, you will have many trials and sorrows. But take heart because I have overcome the world. (John 16:33 NLT)

Jesus assures us that He would be with us through it all and reminds us that He has overcome the world.

You cannot run away from life's challenges. They come to us in different ways and shades. Life will test our resilience in one way of the other. I tell you; everyone will face it. Some worse than others irrespective of status, race, nationality and so on. How you respond is what matters.

Paul also encourages us to continually stay strong even when we are experiencing pain, trials, and hardship. He affirms us with these words:

And we know that all things work together for good to those who love God, to those who are called according to His purpose. (Romans 8:28 NKJV)

In our contemporary world, the central idea of making sacrifices, big or small, seems more alien to the present generation and it will only get worse with the generations that follow us.

It takes the hammer of persistence to drive down the nail of success. The road to success runs uphill, so do not expect that you will break any speed records.

Sacrifice comes with change and this change may test your resilience. Will I survive the big change? How will I fit into the new shell? All these considerations must be painful and excruciating, however it is worth it in the long run.

Do you feel that your shell is getting a little too snug? Why not start looking for a new one?

Do you feel drained by staying where you are or having to find something else? Are you dissatisfied where you are right now, but wonder if a new venture would be any better? I have good news for you: you're not in it alone. God is with you and wants the best for you.

For I know the thoughts that I think toward you, says the Lord, thoughts of peace and not of evil, to give you an expected end. (Jeremiah 29:11 NKJV)

However, God wants us not only to believe, but also to do. Our action is required.

Faith + works = success

This equation is true, but it is not as simple as it seems.

The moment you separate the spirit from the body, you will end up with a corpse. Likewise, the moment you separate faith and works. Whenever you get into a tight corner where everything seems to be working against you and you can't hold on a second longer, do not give up. It might just be the time and place for a turnaround.

Work can be painful and not always be comfortable. Pain, though unpleasant, can be a strong motivator and call to action. Discipline never seems pleasant at the time. However, it can produce a harvest of righteousness and peace for those who have been trained by it.

When pain is withdrawn from us, there's a tendency that we grow complacent pushing God aside and becoming self-sufficient. So, what pain does is to remind us of our frailty and limitations. Sometimes, it's through pain that we can submit ourselves entirely to God as it's one way of reminding us of who He truly is.

The good could keep you from God's best. Your comfort zone can keep you from entering God's promises. Don't remain in a rut forever, afraid to leave your comfortable corner because God is always preparing us for something better. Take a little risk. The sky won't fall; it never does.

Recently, I took a risk to buy bitcoin after a long consideration. Believe me, it remained one of the best stocks in portfolio at the time returning about 25 per cent interest within a month before I sold it off. I am not suggesting you should buy into bitcoin. Cryptocurrencies are quite volatile unless you have a high risk appetite and ready to lose or gain big.

The point I am trying to make is that sometimes change is good for our growth. We must be able to recognize when opportunities are beckoning and seize them.

"There's a tide in the affairs of men, which, taken at the flood, leads on to fortune; Omitted, all the voyage of their life, is bound in shallows and in miseries. On such a full sea are we now afloat, and we must take the current when it serves, or lose our venture." –William Shakespeare

Why do people like doing anything? Is it because we cling tenaciously to the known, holding onto familiarity over risk?

Why do we like doing things the same way over and over? Why do we like the routine?

Little wonder, someone wise once said, that the only ones who want change are babies in diapers.

But how can you make an omelette without breaking the egg? Do not be overly scared to leave your comfort zone, which generally we want to remain in. Telling people to get out of their comfort zones is one suggestion that every advisor would easily recommend. However, we are all unique and have been shaped through different life experiences. We have individual approaches in our aversions to change, risk and challenges.

It's imperative that we fully grasp the concept of the comfort zone, which is subjective as there are many variables around it. This makes stepping out of comfort zone different for everyone.

However, remember God's word to Joshua:

Have I not commanded you? Be strong and courageous. Do not be frightened, and do not be dismayed, for the Lord your God is with you wherever you go. (Joshua 1:8 ESV)

For some, it will require that moving out of both the comfort and competence zones into a discomfort to succeed and make a difference. Maneuvering through the zone of discomfort, guidance may be needed as there will be risk involved and with it, comes fear. Ensure your mind is calibrated to high performance to deliver in this new zone.

The time will come that you reach peak performance, the results become fantastic, and you begin to reap the rewards. It is at peak performance that creativity, novelty, innovation and profits lie.

After Adam and Eve disobeyed God by eating the fruit that God commanded them not to eat in the garden of Eden, pain has become part of living in a fallen world. Like Job, it can happen for reasons we may never comprehend. Nonetheless, God has a purpose for you that transcends the pain you endure or sacrifice you make. Embrace the success that comes from sacrifice and don't just fall for simplistic formulars. Sacrifice to grow!

PRAYER POINTS:

1. Father, help me daily to understand that I need to make sacrifice to grow
2. Father, please give me the grace to endure pain that will ultimately produce great gain in the mighty name of Jesus
3. Father, grant me the resilience to hold on and stay strong in moment of pain and change because I know it will result in my ultimate good in the mighty name of Jesus.

NUGGET #8

DO NOT BE OVERLY RIGHTEOUS

Do not be over righteous, neither be overwise — why destroy yourself?(Ecclesiastes 7:16 NIV)

I was taken aback, and a bit puzzled the first time I saw this Scripture. A superficial reading of this passage presents an apparent problem in comprehension.

How can one be overly righteous or wise? I struggled with it until during a Bible study, I asked my pastor to help me out. I thank God for His grace upon Pastor Adeleke Aiku who shed light on it. He started the Bible study with this opening statement, "What makes a man spiritual is the spirit of God in that man."

In other words, without the Spirit of God in a person, they can not be spiritual, nor spirit filled. And if you are not spirit filled, you can not be righteous. We can not be righteous by our own effort without the Holy Spirit.

So is it possible to be too righteous? In 1 Corinthians 1:5-7, the Scripture says Christians excelled in three areas – knowledge of the word of God, speaking and in the gifts of the Spirit. Yet they weren't spiritual.

Be careful not to practice your righteousness in front of others to be seen by them. If you do, you will have no reward from your father in heaven. (Matthew 6:1 NIV)

In your walk with God, apply prudence in acts of righteousness because you could be exaggerating the well-doing.

The Bible forewarns us:

Therefore, let him who thinks he stands take heed lest he fall. (1 Corinthians 10:12 NKJV)

While it is good to reprove those that offend you, don't cast your pearls before swine.

Neither make thyself over-wise. (Ecclesiastes 7:16 KJV)

Do not be overly opinionated and cocky. Don't look to find fault with everything that someone says or does. Don't over index on something trivial and never join others in pounding the table insisting on it's either your way or the highway. Avoid meddling or commenting in other people's matters because you will be setting up yourself to fall. Always remember to be a shrewd student of power. Do not destroy yourself by being overly righteous or overly wise. Even if you are perfect, you should never complain about someone else's peccadillo. This is key!

PRAYER POINTS:

1. Dear Lord, help me each day to understand that being righteous is not about the appearance in front of others rather it is a sincere and humble desire to know and please you in the mighty name of Jesus
2. Father, help me so that I don't consider myself wise in my own heart, but to seek your own wisdom
3. Lord, help me to never judge other people in the mighty name of Jesus

NUGGET #9

SELF CONTROL:
Emotional Intelligence

A man without self-control is like a city broken into and left without walls. (Proverbs 25:28 ESV)

But the fruit of the Spirit is love, joy, peace, patience, kindness, goodness, faithfulness, gentleness, self-control; against such things there is no law. (Galatians 5:22-23 ESV)

Whoever is slow to anger is better than the mighty, and he who rules his spirit than he who takes a city. (Proverbs 16:32 ESV)

Self-control is one of the nine fruits of the Holy Spirit. It is also known as self management in the contemporary world. It is all about how you manage your emotions, behaviours and responses as well as how you control and manage their impact on others. This is what emotional intelligence is all about and it is must-have soft skill in today's business environment. The reason is not far fetched; the workplace involves constant engagement with people, resources and challenges. Even in ministry, it is about people starting from your home to church, working in departments and doing evangelism. You just can't avoid relating with people.

The two most important ingredients of emotional intelligence are self-control and resilience. The first involves controlling yourself and your responses in adverse situations. The second is the ability to bounce back from negative situations. Understanding your emotional state of mind and how you manage yourself physically is important. How you think and act on information available are also required to self-manage. You need discipline and a strong mindset to subdue the urge to react emotionally rather than rationally.

In his best selling book The 7 Habits of Highly Effective People, Stephen Covey distinguishes between our Circle of Concern (things we care about but can't control) and our Circle of Influence (things we care about and can impact).

Let me explain what this means: you can influence your siblings, family members, colleagues/co-workers, classmates, team member and clients etc. You may not be able to control what these people do, but you can influence them depending on the skill sets you possess. The subject of emotional intelligence as it relates to management in an organization will be dealt with in greater detail in my next book on change management.

And every athlete who goes into training and competes in the games is disciplined and exercises self-control in all things. They do it to win a crown that withers, but we do it to receive an imperishable crown that cannot with. (1 Corinthians 9:25 AMP)

There is no quick and easy way to self-control. It is a process that takes time and effort to master.

Fitness trainers will tell you that it takes self-discipline and self-control to be a winner. During every Olympic Games, it's the athletes who practice well, investing time and resources beforehand, who win gold medals.

Here is the spiritual nugget: Olympic athletes train for years to get a chance to win a moment of glory. But the race we are running is far more important than any earthly athletic event. Self-control is not optional for Christians. It's a must-have.

Why is this so important as a believer? Since you do not live on the moon, where you have no one to relate with, you must find ways to build resilience and stay on top of your game spiritually and physically. Take control of whatever you can and let go of what you can't. Always find ways to lighten up your life as this is important in your walk with Christ. Practice a healthy and balanced lifestyle to manage yourself when you're under stress or when someone pushes your buttons. This allows you to stay disciplined when approaching issues without letting emotions get in the way.

If a brother in the church, a colleague at a workplace or a classmate in school behaves in a way that is negative toward you, try to not see it as a personal attack. Rather, give it time and play it safe by assuming that this person probably has a lot going on that must have spurred the negative behaviour. Especially if it's coming from a brother or sister in Christ, assume the person did it with no malice.

Emotions can be compared to a well crafted violin. When the strings are perfectly tuned right, the result is an amazing song. Violins are environment sensitive and delicate and it doesn't take much for its music to get distorted. Any variations in the surroundings such as humidity, temperature or wind speed may render it off pitch and out-of-tune. Whenever a violin is beautifully played, the listener hears a beautiful melody and pleasurable outcome. On the other hand, if the violin is being played by a rookie with even a subtle change in the surroundings, it can negatively distort the sound and produce unpleasant music.

This is somewhat how the natural man's emotions are wired. But if we let Holy Spirit dwell in us and help us to manage our emotions, the end results are rewarding to us and pleasing to God.

People who are close to me know that I am interested in the round leather game that has tribal marks, that is soccer (football). I have been a Liverpool fan for many years now, having studied in Liverpool, United Kingdom. However, as much as I support Liverpool Football Club, I always distance myself from any emotion in conversation about The club. If I must respond, I do it in such a manner that I don't get drawn into arguments.

But I say to you that for every idle word men may speak, they will give account of it in the day of judgment. (Matthew 12:36 NKJV)

Words matter and how we use ours offers evidence of where we stand before God. The Scripture tells us:

Brood of vipers! How can you, being evil, speak good things? For out of the abundance of the heart the mouth speaks. (Matthew 12:34 NKJV)

Always ask the Holy Spirit to fill your heart with His love, peace, joy and kindness so that it overflows from your mouth. Ask the Holy Spirit to control your tongue so that every word that you speak brings life, heals, builds up and doesn't tear down.

With the help of the Holy Spirit, you too can be like King David:

I have resolved that my mouth will not sin. (Psalm 17:3 NIV)

The ability to speak is a tremendous blessing from God. However, knowing when and what to say is crucial. You must learn to control your emotions and discipline your tongue because speaking can have its downside. As true Christians, our faith in Christ Jesus should impact how we live out our everyday lives, and our emotions as well as our tongues are no exception to that.

Fill your heart and mouth with God's Word so they will overflow with righteousness.

PRAYER POINTS:

1. Father, help me to exercise self-control and help me to control my emotions.
2. Lord teach me to always tame my tongue in the mighty name of Jesus
3. Father, do not let my emotions bubble over when I am angry and help me so that I will not bring disrepute to your name through my speech and actions in the mighty name of Jesus

NUGGET #10

VIRTUE SIGNALING:
Intention and Public Approval

But the Lord said to Samuel,

"Do not consider his appearance or his height, for I have rejected him. The Lord does not look at the things people look at. People look at the outward appearance, but the Lord looks at the heart." – (1 Samuel 16:7 NIV)

Someone once said,

"The secrecy of our charity is one good evidence of its sincerity." – Anonymous

When people post charitable gift photos or receipts on the social media to show how generous they are, that is a textbook definition of virtue signaling.

What difference does it make when a sister whether overtly or covertly, criticizes another sister's indecent dress in the church on a Sunday service just to appear religious but wears something immodest during the week to her workplace, or to a party?

Isn't that the height of hypocrisy?

You must keep your charitable activities secret as much as possible. Stop signaling your virtues to others to seek public or self-justification.

Virtue signaling is self-promoting and sometimes censorious and when we signal our virtues to the public, we undercut our blessings and rewards. Jesus warns us to not exalt ourselves.

Whose approval do you seek? A pastor, the department head in the church or that of the congregation? How about the approval of your parents, spouse or children? Or maybe it's your boss or followers on social media?

In Matthew 6, Jesus was teaching the Sermon on the Mount and he rebukes the Pharisees. Self-seeking, self-righteous, cocky and conceited, they were religious leaders parading around in the synagogues in their spiritual garb to be seen by men. Funny enough, the Pharisees were doing the right things: fasting, praying, and giving of alms, but it was all for the wrong motive.

Beware of practicing your righteousness before other people in order to be seen by them, for then you will have no reward from your Father who is in heaven. (Matthew 6:1 ESV)

And when you pray, you must not be like the hypocrites. For they love to stand and pray in the synagogues and at the street corners, that they may be seen by others. (Matthew 6:5 ESV)

Why would Jesus call them hypocrites? That was because in their praying and fasting, they were basically seeking the praise of men even though they appeared to be treasuring and honouring God.

Why would someone take beautiful spiritual disciplines like praise, prayer or preaching and exploit them by seeking self-glorification? Why would someone turn a philanthropic act of charity into a self-serving activity? Seeking human applause is a cistern that does not hold water.

Human minds are so sinful that we can alter the most basic tenets of worship to God and twist the purest of activities and turn them into something that conjures approval and praise from people around us.

Doing evangelism or leading prayer meetings or worshipping God to be noticed is the first sign that you're doing the right thing for the wrong reasons. That praise from your pastor or church member is usually temporal and fleeting. Only God's approval lasts forever.

Why do we go about telling people how much effort, time and energy we have invested into a project in our church?

Why do we use an opportunity for public prayer to draw unnecessary attention to ourselves?

What's your intention and whose approval matters to you?

As a leader entrusted with the authority to pick or nominate group members for an event or activity in a much larger group, why do we discriminate?

Have you been given any responsibility at your workplace or in the church and you have subtly turned it into a personal vendetta?

Have you been entrusted with the power to schedule people at work or in the church setting and you're misusing it to malign or get back at someone?

Have you succeeded in weaponizing your authority or position in the church and using it to get at perceived enemies or persons you consider not in your camp?

Why are you so keen in buying that big house by the riverside even when its financial implication is out of your reach?

Why are you often fixated on dressing ostentatiously in designer clothes?

Why are you posting those photos on Facebook or Meta as it is called now? Perhaps, it's to attract a million likes or show off our wealth.

What are the motives behind what you are doing?

Always remember, that on the last day every piece of our work including our motives shall be tested by fire. The question we need to ask ourselves is "would what I am doing right now survive the test of that fire?

I tell you; they have received their reward in full. (Matthew 6:5b NIV)

As far as Jesus was concerned, these Pharisees would have no reward.

John puts it like this:

For they loved praise of men more than the praise of God. (John 12:43 KJV)

Why are we so concerned about impressing others? While there's nothing wrong in getting approval of certain persons in our lives – especially from our spiritual leaders and pastors – the motive must be for the right reasons. And God's approval must always come first.

Apostle Paul hits the nail on the head when he says:

So we speak, not to please man, but to please God who tests our hearts. (1 Thessalonians 2:4 ESV)

Anyone who loves their father or mother more than me is not worthy of me; anyone who loves their son or daughter more than me is not worthy of me. (Matthew 10:37 NIV)

Am I now trying to win the approval of human beings, or of God? Or am I trying to please people? If I were still trying to please people, I would not be a servant of Christ. (Galatians 1:10 NIV)

Paul says it is wrong to seek men's praise and even more wrong to put pleasing humans first before pleasing God. Not even pleasing your pastor should come before pleasing

God. Shun the desire for the applause of men and any form of self-glorification.

Let's allow the Holy Spirit to make us more like Jesus, who loved us unconditionally and gave Himself as a ransom for us. That day shall come when we'll experience the smile of His approval. That is the approval of the only One who matters. Do not be an approval addict.

I know this sounds bizarre in a world where social media is the order of the day. Facebook (Meta) is now like getting a seat at the lunch table with all the cool children in the insane asylum isn't it? For those of us with Twitter account, if someone favourites our tweet, we get a star, don't we? We literally compete for the number of likes we get per post in a bid to get people to approve of us.

Be introspective to see if you have got any Pharisee in you or your ministry. Do not struggle to win the approval of men rather than God. Only one glance will count for eternity. The process of seeking God's approval begins with a willingness to cultivate the attitude of praising God from our hearts to transform our minds.

Identifying with Jesus often comes with a price. Sometimes the cost can be high, and it varies from one believer to another. Persecution, jeering, name calling, lost of opportunities, peer pressure, cancel culture and much more. Even in recent times, people still face persecution and peer pressures forcing them to conceal their faith in God.

Don't get discouraged and lose your steam. Whatever the cost, don't backdown or sit on the fence.

The story about Elijah and prophets of Baal in 1 King 18 gives us something to learn. After three and half years without rain, Elijah told Ahab to assemble the people of Israel on Mount Carmel along with the 450 prophets of Baal. While they were dilly-dallying, Elijah approach them and said,

How long will you go limping between two different opinions? If the Lord is God, follow Him; but if Baal, then follow him. (1 Kings 18:21 ESV)

And the Bible tells us that the people did not answer him a word.

In Christ Jesus, there's no vacillating. No being neutral. Being a disciple is voluntary but once you have made that choice to follow Him, then there's no room for humming and harring.

Don't bother about what others may say about you when it comes to your commitment to Jesus. Don't play hid your position or where you stand when it matters.

But …they would not openly acknowledge their faith for fear they would be put out of the synagogue. (John 12:42 NIV)

God dislikes indecision and those who sit on the fence. In God's Kingdom, there's a need to take decision and stand for something. If you don't stand for something, you will fall for everything.

Speaking to the church in Laodicea, the Scripture says,

I know your works, that you are neither cold nor hot. I could wish you were cold or hot. (Revelation 3:15 NKJV)

Craving human praise is a cistern that doesn't just work when it comes to walking with God. Jesus is the answer. He is the only living water and only in Him will we never thirst. Stand firm, be resolute and unswerving. Identify with Christ and become a disciple who seeks God's approval over human praise.

PRAYER POINTS:

1. Father, please transform my mind so that I will seek Your approval first and not seek the approval of those around me or to desire their praise in Jesus' name
2. Dear Lord, I often find myself slipping into the trap of using the world's criteria to evaluate success and failure. Help me to take my eyes off the things that impress people and fix them on the things that are truly important to You. Lord, help me to lift my eyes to heaven, to the One who truly loves me in the mighty name of Jesus.
3. Father, only Your approval matters to me. Help me to renew my mind with Your unchanging truth. Please help me to always seek Your approval and not the approval of men in the mighty name of Jesus.

NUGGET #11

DISTRACTION

Distraction, at least the dangerous kind I am talking about in this book, shifts one's attention from something of greater importance to something of lesser importance. Our fundamental and most dangerous problem is being distracted from God. We shift our attention from the greatest person in existence to countless lesser things. The Bible calls this idolatry.

Since the fall of man in the garden of Eden, humans have struggled with staying focused. To make issues worse, we live in an age of unprecedented distraction and noise. Experts in this field are seeing the negative effects this is having on humans. Many of us feel it: the buzzing brain, the attention atrophy, the diminishing tolerance for praying and meditating on the Word of God.

We are becoming conditioned to distraction and it is beginning to harm our mental capacity to listen and think carefully. To be still, to hear His small still voice, to pray and to meditate are becoming lost. This is a spiritual danger, an evil from which we need God's deliverance.

Distraction becomes idolatry at some point. When we are regularly distracted by something, our attention often runs to what is important to us thereby revealing what we truly cherish. Distraction reveals the idols we love.

This happened to Jesus's friend, Martha, who was busy in the kitchen while Jesus taught her sister in her home. Martha complained that her sister Mary wasn't helping because she was sitting at His feet and Jesus was clear:

And Jesus answered and said to her, Martha, Martha, you are worried and troubled about many things. But one thing is needed, and Mary has chosen that good part, which will not be taken away from her. (Luke 10:41-42 NKJV)

Martha was distracted from Jesus by things that weren't important Why? Because she was anxious about feeding everyone.

"You can be zealous in the wrong thing." –Pastor Adeleke Aiku

Martha was zealous and anxious in the wrong thing at least at the time. Martha was probably anxious about what everyone would think of her if she wasn't a good host.

She forgot that God is not nearly as interested in our efficiency as He is in our faith. Martha didn't realize she was distracted until Jesus pointed it out to her. All along, Martha thought she was doing the right thing by serving. But Jesus was quick to point out that her values were disordered and that she had shifted her focus from the greater importance to the lesser.

Distraction is a reminder of our human frailty and limits that we are not God and are not infallible. Since we are prone to unjustifiable and ridiculous, levels of pride, this can be very good for us. Distraction is humbling, forcing us to ask God for the help we so desperately desire.

Distraction can build our faith. Do you remember how God let enemies mock and intimidate Nehemiah and his Jerusalem wall-builders, slowing down the work in Nehemiah 4:1-23.

Sometimes, God lets us battle inefficient distractions to build our dependence on Him. If you're a Christian who, for whatever reason, has a more difficult struggle with distraction, you need not feel condemned.

Therefore, there is now no condemnation (no adjudging guilty of wrong) for those who are in Christ Jesus, who live and walk not after the dictates of the flesh, but after the dictates of the Spirit. (Romans 8:1 AMP)

Good stewardship looks like fighting distraction as best as you possibly can. Push yourself. You may not be able to do what others can do, but God will hold you accountable for the measure of grace given to you.

Having gifts, faculties, talents, qualities that differ according to the grace given us, let us use them: He whose gift is prophesy, let him prophesy according to the proportion of his faith. (Romans 12:6 AMP).

Begin to see certain distractions as evils. Don't allow anyone pull you into any form of debate or argument whether it's political, religious or apolitical. An argument that doesn't resolve anything, but rather leaves you emotionally, mentally and physically drained should be avoided.

Distractions are part of the world we live in, but as believers, we must always stay focused because no one knows when the trumpet shall sound. We must be at our duty post doing exactly what we are called to do. It doesn't matter whether it's your studies, secular workplace or marriage as long as it has the propensity to impact your personal relationship with God.

Nehemiah stayed focused during seasons of noise and distractions, rebuilding the broken wall of Jerusalem while Sanballat and Tobiah did everything possible to distract him. Nehemiah never took his eyes off the ball. He repeatedly sent them the same message each time they tried.

So, I replied by sending this message to them: "I am engaged in a great work, so I can't come. Why should I stop working to come and meet with you?" (Nehemiah 6:3 NLT)

Anytime you get distracted by other people's opinions or you allow yourself to be dragged into unnecessary debates instead of seeking the mind of Christ, you are coming down your wall. Never let anyone's opinion loom larger than God in your life. In those seasons, lean deeper into God's Word, praise and worship, prayer and fasting. Keep laying those bricks that will eventually form the pillars holding your walls from collapsing.

Remember, not every battle requires your response.

Let us relate it with the analogy of the eagle and raven. The only bird that dares to peck an eagle is the raven. It sits on the eagle's back and bites their neck. However, the eagle doesn't respond and never fights back. The eagle does not spend its time and energy on the raven.

All the eagle does is open its wings, begin to flap and up it flies even higher in the sky. The higher the flight, the harder and uncomfortable it becomes for the raven to breathe. The eagle keeps flying higher and the raven eventually falls to the ground due to lack of oxygen. Ultimately, the raven suffers from a condition known as hypoxia, an extreme shortage of oxygen.

There are lessons we can learn from the story of the eagle and the raven.

- Not all battles require your input or response
- Not all arguments or critics you need to respond to or answer back

Just lift your hands, raise your voice, point your face high unto the heavens and your critics will fall away. However, ensure those hands that are being lifted are holy.

In the Old Testament, King Hezekiah was faced with a real crisis: the city of Jerusalem was under siege. The Israelites were confronted with psychological warfare at the wall and were inundated with discouraging threats from the Syrian army commander.

Well, guess what the king did?

But the people were silent and did not utter a word because Hezekiah had commanded them, "Do not answer him." (2 Kings 18:36 NLT)

He ordered his subordinates at the wall to not answer the adversary, a wise thing to do in the face of intimidation and mockery. Isn't it?

You don't have to react or respond to every criticism or anything that the world throws at you. And you know why?

Do not be afraid or discouraged...For the battle is not yours, but God's. (2 Chronicles 20:15 NIV).

The Bible tells us in 2 Kings 19:1-14 that the first thing King Hezekiah did to show he was upset was to put on sackcloth and go into the temple twice. After that, he sent for the prophet Isaiah. The king asked the prophet to plead with God for intervention. For this king, it was prophet Isaiah, but for us in this present time, it is the Bible, God's Word.

That is exactly what we need when we face crisis. Stay focused and seek God's face and be rest assured of God's intervention. We can take a leaf from King Hezekiah's approach (as well as the eagle). It is right to for us to view certain distractions as evils because they waste precious time.

Time, of course, is like a tax we pay, for which there's no refund.

Distraction keeps you away from achieving your goal and productivity remains the key to staving off any such distraction. Set timelines and align yourself with the goals you want to accomplish. Don't let distraction come in the way. You're the most important factor determining your own failure or success. Be in the driver's seat of your life. No one has the right to truncate your dreams. Not distraction!

PRAYER POINTS:

1. Dear Lord, protect me from every form of distraction and whatever it takes, Lord, increase my resolve to pursue only what You call me to do in the mighty name of Jesus.

2. Father, deliver me from distractions, oppositions, obstacles and mountains or strong holds that may want to hinder me from reaching my goal in Jesus' name.

3. Lord, take away every form of distraction in my life and help me to focus on what truly matters in the mighty name of Jesus.

MANAGE TIME AND END PROCRASTINATION

To everything there is a season, and a time to every purpose under the heaven. A time to be born, and a time to die; a time to plant, and a time to pluck up that which is planted...A time to get and a time to lose; a time to keep, and a time to cast away; A time to rend, and a time to sew; a time to keep silence, and a time to speak; A time to love, and a time to hate; a time of war, and a time of peace. (Ecclesiastes 3:1-8 KJV)

Of the sons of Issachar who had understanding of the times. (1 Chronicles 12:32 NKJV)

"There's a tide in the affairs of men which, taken at the flood leads unto fortune." -William Shakespeare

These are some of my opinions:

- After salvation, time is the next most important thing to mankind
- The unit of destiny is time
- Not all seasons carry equal possibilities
- Time is an investment

Time and seasons are God's gifts to man. But it is our choice how we invest our time. There is a time and season for every activity under the sun. Each day has 24 hours, that is 1,440 minutes, or 86,400 seconds in each day that we have got to make investment and how we use it depends entirely on us.

There's no rollover time. Let's imagine there's a financial institution that credits your cheque account at 12 a.m. every morning. But it carries over zero balance. Any unused amount is wiped off and deletes to zero balance at 11:59 p.m. every evening. What would you do?

The answer is straightforward: you'd draw out every penny or cent to have zero balance or lose it. Everyone of you has such a bank account. The name of that bank is time.

Every morning, the bank of time credits us with 86,400 seconds or 1,440 minutes. Every night, it writes off whatever remainder of that time we failed to use or invest to good purpose. Any unused time is deleted.

There are no rollover seconds and it allows no overdraft. Every morning, it opens a new account for you and at exactly 11:59 p.m., it deletes whatever remains of the time. Any day you fail to utilize the full day's deposit of 1,440 minutes, the loss is yours. No rollover, no compensation and no drawing against future deposits.

You cannot draw against tomorrow that has not come and you must live in the now on today's deposits only. This means that you need to live in the present without recourse to past or future deposits. No living in the past, no living in the future.

You are expected to invest your 1,440 minutes each day to maximize your returns. These returns will have to cut across all portfolios. You must use it to generate maximum returns on your goal, career, health, marriage, success, happiness, and well being. What will you do? The clock is tickling and running. Maximize it because time of the essence.

Don't steal or squander your employer's time at your workplace. An employer pays you to work for a specified period and when you use that time for something outside of the overall organization's objectives, then you're a thief. Always endeavour to use your breaks for prayer, phone calls or any other personal commitments.

"Do not squander time, for it is the stuff life is made of." - Benjamin Franklin

Everyone lives by the clock because time is of the essence and a valuable commodity to humans.

"Work expands so as to fill the time available for its completion." - C. Northcote Parkinson

I heard this quote a few years ago while I was working in the banking sector. It heightened my awareness and I have seen it at play in organizations in the West and in my country of birth. Parkinson's Law, as it's popularly known, proposes that people will subconsciously fill the time available for any work or task.

Avoid a mindset that sabotages focus and performance. Some people appear busy but are totally ineffective. They are busy filling in time, running the clock and killing time. What a fool does in the end, the wise man does in the beginning. Prolonged idleness paralyzes initiatives.

So, teach us to number our days, that we may apply our hearts unto wisdom. (Psalm 90:12 KJV)

God wants you to treasure each day and number it like He does. Your time here on earth is brief, shorter than we even know.

You sweep them away as with a flood; they are like a dream, like grass that is renewed in the morning: in the morning it flourishes and is renewed; in the evening it fades and withers. (Psalm 90:5-6 ESV)

The passage gives us some perspectives on how short our grass-like lives seem. We can expect 70 or 80 years on this earth if we are healthy, but even our best years will bring trouble and sorrow. Suddenly our time is up, and we disappear.

Take note of the lyrics in this song:

If I could save time in a plastic bottle
The first thing that I'd like to do
Is to save every day till eternity passes away
Just to spend them with you

Jim Croce was a singer/songwriter who was beginning to ride the wave of international fame. He was a young father whose heart was full of love for his one-year-old boy, but his music career demanded much of his time. Touring and other commitments took him away from his only son more than he was around for him, and this was a hard pill to swallow. Jim could feel the brief irretrievable time he had to enjoy with his son frittering away. In an attempt to display his fatherly longing, he wrote "Time In a Bottle".

In the song's chorus, Jim expressed an angst many of us can relate to:

There never seems to be enough time
To do the things you want to do
Once you find them.

Jim knew he didn't have eternity to be around his son. But he had a far less time than he knew. Unfortunately, a few months after he wrote this song, Jim died. He was tragically killed on September 21, 1973, in a plane crash in Natchitoches, Louisiana. Jim was 30 years old.

Live your life every day as if that is the last day of your life. To help us fully grasp the concept of time, let's look at what each letter represents in TIME.

T = Treasure
I = Invest
M = Manage
E = Enjoy

Treasure: Time is a commodity and resource and should be treasured. The Scripture admonishes us to treasure time as valuable.

- If you want to know the value of a split second, ask the Olympic 400-meter athlete who missed qualifying by a four-tenths of a second
- If you want to know the value of a second, ask the man who just had a very near miss and barely missed a head on with an oncoming SUV at speeding at 160 kilometres per hour
- If you want to know the value of a minute, ask the woman who just had a heart attack while she was dining in a restaurant and a paramedic was at the next table and saved her life with CPR
- If you want to know the value of one hour, ask the businessperson whose flight had just been delayed by 60 minutes making him late for a crucial meeting
- If want to know the value of one day, ask the man whose heart is failing and requires emergency surgery, but his surgeon is on vacation and not returning to work until tomorrow
- If you want to know the value of one month, ask as a woman who just had a stillbirth in her second trimester
- If you want to know the value of one year, ask a final year medical student who just failed his clinical exams

Time is unquestionably a precious and priceless commodity so appreciate every moment that you live. Yesterday is gone and it is history. Tomorrow is a mystery and unknown. Today is a gift and that is why it is called the present.

In Canada, like in many other western nations, I hear people say this all the time:

"Time is money."

This is not exactly true. You can always make more money, but you can't create more time. Time is the unit of destiny and should be treasured as the most important asset on earth and in the balance sheet of your life.

Invest: You can't save time, but you can invest it and put it into proper use to reap its reward. While money can be saved, you can't save time. like money, time can be spent and invested. But if you don't use it, you lose it forever and this makes time more valuable than money. How you invest your time tells where what your priorities are.

For where your treasure is, there will your heart be also. (Matthew 6:21 KJV)

There are 168 hours in each week. The average person spends 40 of those hours working and another 10 of those hours commuting to work and running errands. About 24 of those hours are spent on eating and personal hygiene, and the average person spends 56 hours sleeping. This leaves us with about 38 hours of free or uncommitted hours, which adds up to 5.5 hours every day. How you invest this time reveals what you are really interested in.

Imagine if your pastor was to trail you for a week to discover what you do with those 5.5 hours every day. I can only guess what they might observe. The pastor would see that most people are most interested in social media and surfing the internet, followed closely by playing video games and watching television. Studying or reading would top the priority list for others.

How many of those free hours are being invested in prayer, studying God's Word and personal quiet time?

Manage: Time is a gift from God and how we use it matters. Our stewardship to God will be judged on how we utilize this gift. We must figure out our priorities and place them in the right order or else other things will take their place in our lives. How do we spend our uncommitted time? Spending time with family, or friends or with God?

Why do you think the corporate world spends huge amounts of money and resources in training, seminars and workshops on time management?

One of the leading experts in the field of time management is Stephen Covey, author of the bestseller 7 Habits of Highly Effective People

"Time management is a misleading concept. You can't really manage time. You can't delay it, speed it up, save it or lose it," says Covey. "No matter what you, do time keeps moving forward at the same rate. The challenge is not to manage time but to manage ourselves." – Stephen Covey

Instead of time management, the Scripture talks about redeeming the time.

Redeeming the time because the days are evil. (Ephesians 5:16 KJV)

People are like grass; their beauty is like a flower in the field. The grass withers and the flower fades. (1 Peter 1:24 NLT)

The brevity of human existence and the shortness of time is what science has never been able to overcome. Rather than concentrating on the preciousness of time, scientists are busy trying to figure out how to gain more time. They obsessively seek ways to beat what they cannot create using drugs, creams, food and lifestyles.

See then that you walk circumspectly, not as fools, but as wise, redeeming the time, because the days are evil. (Ephesians 5:16 NKJV)

Time is finite for us whether we accept it or not. It's not ours and we can not add to what we have, because it constantly moves forward at the same rate. All that is in heaven and earth belongs to God and we are nothing but stewards.

Let a man so account of us, as of the ministers of Christ, and stewards of the mysteries of God. (1 Corinthians 4:1 KJV)

We must be good stewards of time as we are in all other things given to us by God.

Engage: To enjoy your time here, spend time wisely to engage with God, His people, family and loved ones.

No one on their deathbed ever said they wished they'd spent more time on social media.

This very minute can never be recalled. Today is special and God has given it to us as a present. One day will be your last day. One breath will be your last.

However, be vigilant when you engage with your community. Consider those moments you have engaged with others in a family, congregation, class, or sports team discussing things which are of no eternal value. How many minutes or hours of our lives have we spent in the presence of friends and loved ones talking about worldly things with more vigour and zeal than we do with the Word?

While engaging with others is a good idea, sometimes the benefits are small. Yes, there can be an element of redeeming the time whenever we commune with one another. But what purpose does it have if you've redeemed time from the world only to act and spend it with people close to you like the world does.

Engaging with people generally brings little redemption. I encourage you to consider what exactly it is that you are doing with people when you're with them. Try to put aside the silly and mundane things of the world and actively engage with one another over things that truly matter. Work at having conversations that point toward Scripture. Scriptural meditation is a sure-fire way to redeem time and necessary when you're trying to turn from worldly and frivolous pursuits.

I'm not trying to make anyone feel guilty. There were times that I found myself in the same swamp and stuck in the same mire. So I'm writing to you and myself as well. The point is to consider how you spent your time daily. It isn't to pronounce a minimum number of hours you must spend thinking about God to be considered righteous. It doesn't work that way. You can think and talk about God for 1,440 minutes each day and still not be righteous. This is a war against our nature, not a guilt trip on anyone.

Time, of course, is like a tax we pay, for which there's no refund. Lost money can be found but lost time is lost forever. Time spent means you have less to spend. Every distracted 60 seconds is an unrecoverable minute, now frozen in the permanent past. It is right to seek to make the best use of our time in these evil days.

Making the best use of your time because the times are evil. (Ephesians 5:16 ESV)

"Don't stand shivering upon the bank; plunge in at once and have it over." -Sam Slick

Watch your time. The clock is always running!

PRAYER POINTS:

1. Father, please help me to manage my time properly. Send your Holy Spirit to help me achieve a good balance in all that I must juggle daily.
2. Father, may I not abandon to study your Word because of work. Help me to not get distracted by social media. Let no aspect of my life suffer due to time mismanagement.
3. Father, help me to end procrastination. From today, help me to do what needs to be done while I still can in the mighty name of Jesus.

WALK IN THE SPIRIT: THE NUMERO UNO

This isn't just another nugget. This is the numero uno without which, it's practically and humanly impossible to please God in this fallen world.

I'm thankful that my Zonal Pastor Adeleke Aiku is a great teacher of the Word. He helped me understand walking in the Spirit during a Bible study series on The Spiritual Man.

I say then: Walk in the Spirit, and you shall not fulfil the lust of the flesh. (Galatians 5:16 NKJV)

What does it really mean to walk in the Spirit?

Firstly, let us understand some concepts such as walk, Spirit and flesh.

The word walk is a verb because it is an action word. To walk is simply to move along or move at a regular pace by setting down each foot in turn and never having both feet off the ground. So, when you walk, you move from one point to another. However, in the scriptural context, it is often used as metaphor to denote practical daily living.

Flesh is the soft epidermis tissues or substance which covers the bones and is permeated with blood. Flesh refers to the physical earthly body.

You clothed me with skin and flesh, and you knit my with bones and sinews together. (Job 10:11 NLT)

Flesh is also the biblical expression for the dwelling place of everything in a person that opposes God and His will.

As offspring of Adam, we inherit the fleshly nature of man, but believers are given a new life in Christ which is subject to the Holy Spirit. It is our inborn flesh or Adam nature that urges us to yield to evil desires. Flesh is mortal and naturally susceptible to malady, pain and fatigue over time.

Have you ever wondered why dogs don't go to church, why cats don't worship, donkeys don't have morning devotion and chickens don't sing? Even animals that scientists claim to share close relationships to humans like monkeys and chimpanzees don't sing hymns. Only human beings can do all these things and the reason is simple.

And God said, Let us make man in our own image, after our likeness: and let them have dominion over the fish of the sea, and over the cattle, and over every creeping thing that creepeth upon the earth. (Genesis 1:26 KJV)

God is Spirit, and those who worship Him must worship in spirit and truth. (John 4:24 NKJV)

Unlike the creatures of this earth, humans are spirit beings. Apostle Paul affirmed this assertion when he wrote:

And may your spirit and soul and body be kept healthy and faultless until the Lord Jesus Christ returns. (1 Thessalonians 5:23 CEV)

The spirit in us is what orients us to God and it's the part of us that constantly communicates and relates to our maker, God.

Now that we have got a grasp of what it means to walk, the basic concept of the flesh and Spirit, let's examine what it means to walk in the Spirit.

The very moment after you give your life to Jesus Christ and experience the new birth, you move from death to life and begin your Christian walk. To walk in the Spirit simply means to allow Jesus Christ through the Holy Spirit to direct the way you live your life. To walk in the Spirit means that you are living a life that is guided by Him daily.

This I say then, Walk in the Spirit, and ye shall not fulfill the lust of the flesh. (Galatians 5:16 KJV)

And now you Gentiles have also heard the truth, the Good News that God saves you. And when you believed in Christ, He identified you as His own by giving you the Holy Spirit, whom He promised long ago. (Ephesians 1:13 NLT)

When we give our lives to Christ, the Holy Spirit makes His dwelling place inside of us.

And because you are sons, God has sent forth the Spirit of his Son into your hearts, crying out, Abba, Father! (Galatians 4:6 NKJV)

The reason God sends the Holy Spirit is to help us in our walk with God. To walk in the Spirit is to walk in the new life of Christ through faith. This also means to balk at any old life of sin and bondage. By walking in the Spirit, you become preoccupied with the person of Christ. The secret of the Christian life is to walk in the Spirit by allowing Jesus Christ through the work of the Holy Spirit to live in and through us by the power of His resurrection.

To walk in the Spirit, we first need to receive the Holy Spirit, the actual force that is as real as an elevator lifting us from ground zero to 10th floor. It is nearly impossible to lead a life of holiness without the Holy Spirit.

The more I try to live the life of a true disciple in Christ using my own human effort, the harder it is. If the Christian life looks hard, remember that we are not called to live it by ourselves. It is so uncomplicated that we tend to stumble over its simplicity, and it is difficult because it is a spiritual life that only Jesus Christ can enable us to live.

When we walk in the Spirit, the desires of our flesh are rejected, and we need to refuse to give in to its demands. It is to spend and be spent in the abundant life of Jesus Christ through the leading of the Holy Spirit.

Through the indwelling of the Holy Spirit in us, we are able to subdue the fleshly desires of sin and lead a holy life of a true disciple. This is the work that the Holy Spirit does when we walk in the Spirit.

Each believer deals with warfare in their minds each day, but God has given them the willpower to choose which direction they want to yield to. We can choose to walk in the flesh or walk in the Spirit. It is entirely our choice.

For the desires of the flesh are against the Spirit, and the desires of the Spirit are against the flesh. For these are opposed to each other, to keep you from doing the things you want to do. (Galatians 5:17 ESV)

Every second, every minute and every hour of the day, we face warfare between Spirit and our flesh, and it is up to us to decide which of them wins.

Stay Plugged in 24/7: Staying connected to God every day of the week is the only way you can walk in the spirit successfully. The flesh is in constant opposition to the Spirit and you will find that when your Spirit is willing to pray, the flesh wants to nap. When the Spirit is willing to fast, the flesh wants to eat and drink. There's always a war waging inside of us pulling us in opposing directions: to follow the leading of the Holy Spirit or succumb to our sinful fleshly desires. This war has always been there and will never cease until we behold His face in glory.

I used to wonder why God didn't remove sinful desires from a believer the moment one is born again because I know God can do it if he wants . Perhaps God wants to us to be continually mindful of our sinfulness and weaknesses or remind us of our frailty and mortality to keep us constantly dependent on Him for daily survival.

Why is it important to walk in the Spirit when we have been told that the flesh is as good as dead and its doom is certain? Because there are outlying pockets of resistance and the guerrillas of our flesh don't want to give up the fight. It keeps fighting back through its desires. The main purpose of walking in the Spirit is to conquer the flesh.

Now the works of the flesh are manifest, which are these; adultery, fornication, uncleanness, lasciviousness, idolatry, witchcraft, hatred, variance, emulations, wrath, strife, seditions, heresies, envying, murder, drunkenness, revelling, and such. (Galatians 5:19-21 KJV)

Flesh or Holy Spirit? The winner depends on which one we yield to. If we yield to the flesh, fleshly desires manifest. If we yield to the Spirit, we shall bear the fruits of the Holy Spirit.

We receive the impact of the Holy Spirit's indwelling depending on the measure and degree of our yielding. The more we yield, the more the impact and the less we yield the less the impact. So in order not to get disconnected and starved of the nutrients that the Holy Spirit supplies, we must stay plugged in 24/7.

Efforts to ensure we are walking daily in the Spirit should be deliberate and concerted. Confirm the ever-increasing presence of the fruit of the Spirit daily. Aim for a growing conversational relationship with God all through the day.

When reviewing your day look for a reduction in sin's appeal and a growing ability to discern God's guidance.

Walking in the Spirit allows us to look at things from a spiritual perspectives. Our response to situations should be with God in mind. When we are faced with challenges, when we meet people, in our conversations and in our daily lives, we must seek ways to grow deeper spiritually in our walk with God. Don't throw your hands up in despair when problems mount, instead pray and seek the will of God through the Holy Spirit.

We should continually allow the Holy Spirit to guide us in doing the Father's will, and engage in those things that will help us build our faith in the Lord. Meditate on this prayer by Apostle Paul:

And now the God of peace…make you complete in every good work to do His will, working in you what is well pleasing in His sight, through Jesus Christ, to whom be glory forever and ever. Amen. (Hebrews 13:20-21 NKJV)

And if it is indeed the Holy Spirit who works in us what is pleasing in God's sight, then we must ask Him to give us a brand new heart and transform us with a right spirit.

Create in me a clean heart, O God, and renew a right spirit within me. (Psalm 51:10 KJV)

I encourage you to stay plugged in and strong in God. Seek Him wholeheartedly daily. If there is anything that I regret today, it is not seeking God earlier in life.

I love those who love me; And those who seek me early and diligently will find me. (Proverbs 8:17 AMP)

Ways to Stay Connected: If you seek and find God early in your walk with Him, your life will be a success. Imagine finding God as a teenager when you have nothing but time to engage with Him? When nothing worries or disturbs your life other than your studies.

Here are some practical ways you can stay connected in the digital age:

- Download a Bible app on your mobile device and strive to read a chapter or some verses of the Scripture every day. You will be surprised when you are even prompted to read more. Downloading the Bible app on your mobile phone helps you to gain quick access to Scripture while on the go. If you are driving, walking or on transit, it's not always practical to flip open your hard copy Bible. But having the Bible on your mobile device makes it easy to look at a passage that crosses your mind.

Scripture plays an important role in the life of every Christian regardless of how long they have been saved. It is undoubtedly true that what you read impacts you.

All Scripture is given by inspiration of God, and is profitable for doctrine, for reproof, for correction and for instruction in righteousness. (2 Timothy 3:16-17 NKJV)

The Bible is replete with a variety of literature, including hymns, poems, psalms, songs as well as stories and letters.

The Bible is more than a compendium of literature or history or art or science. It tells us about God's nature, who He is and what's on His mind. Reading the Bible every day helps reorient our thinking so He can develop our minds to maturity. It's advisable to read whole biblical books or at least full chapters to avoid misapplication of texts or taking Scripture out of context.

- Devotion should be a daily habit. Another way to stay constantly connected to the leading of the Holy Spirit is to read and study a daily devotional guide. I've found the Open Heaven by Pastor E. A Adeboye to be an amazing daily devotional guide.
- Quiet time is an essential spiritual tool. Set aside time in a certain location to get away, be alone and fellowship with God. Most of us who call ourselves Christians nowadays are weak when compared with the exploits of the early Christians. This is because we often depend on crowds or group activities in place of personal fellowship with God.

If you want God to reveal Himself to you and truly grow in your relationship with Him, wholehearted devotion is essential. Through regular quiet time and wholeheartedness, God transforms us into His likeness. Deliberately devoting time and a place to study as well as setting aside a quiet time to listen to God speak, will draw you nearer to Him. Beyond a deepened friendship with God and new heart, quiet time can help broaden your thinking. Through wholehearted devotion, you will come to know who God is and what it means to be a true child of God.

This is what the Lord says, "Don't let the wise boast in their wisdom, or the powerful boast in their power, or the rich boast in their riches. But those who wish to boast should boast in this alone: that they truly know me and understand that I am the Lord who demonstrates unfailing love and who brings justice and righteousness to the earth, and that I delight in these things. I, the Lord, have spoken!" (Jeremiah 9:23-24 NLT)

How well do you know the Master? Would you recognize Jesus if you accidentally bump into Him at the train station or Walmart or in a grocery store? Would you recognize Him if you encounter Him at the library? God calls you into friendship and to have fellowship with Him so you will know who He is in any situation.

This is my commandment, that you love one another as I have loved you. Greater love has no one than this, than to lay down one's life for his friends. You are my friends if you do whatever I command you. No longer do I call you servants, for a servant does not know what his master is doing; but I have called you friends, for all things that I heard from my Father I have made known to you. (John 15:12-15 NKJV)

It is in this constant fellowship with God that we begin to grow our hatred for sin and learn to love righteousness. Most of my major resolutions concerning any issues are made during my own personal quiet time and devotions.

Let me share a recent experience. After I passed my road test and got my driver's license in Canada, I decided to purchase a car. I had investigated the cost of insurance and price of gas so I had a fair idea of how much it would cost each month to run a car. Meanwhile, my average monthly expense on a bus pass was about C$103. After I got my first car, I went to an insurance office to register it. I quickly realized that my monthly insurance would be almost a third higher than I had envisioned.

I told some of my Christian friends about my monthly insurance, and they suggested my cost was too high. Every single one of the them was paying far less than I was going to pay. I felt cheated and returned to the insurance office to complain .

The agent was sympathetic, but what could she do? She went over the documentation and car registration again. Interestingly, there was one question that is one of the main factors that determines how much money you can save.

That question looks something like this: "Would you be driving the vehicle/car to work more than four times in a month?"

I had responded yes.

The insurance agent suggested that if I had answered no, then my monthly insurance cost would be reduced by the exact equivalent to the difference that I was hoping to get.

The long and the short of it is I would've to lie to get the discount on my monthly insurance cost. This difference was substantial and could cover a portion of my monthly grocery bill. But how could I live with that lie?

In my morning quiet time, God told me that I couldn't alter anything.

The agent repeated the question again and waited for my final answer. I repeated my previous answer and didn't change anything. It was the right thing to do.

I remember going back to one of those friends and telling him without mincing words, that answering no to that question as others probably did would have been a flat out lie. This is just one out of many sacrifices that believers face on daily basis. A loss or a 'waste' of fund you may say.

Imagine that I never had devotion or quiet time on the day that I caught this rhema. I would have probably missed it. Therefore, the importance of spending quality time with God cannot be over emphasized.

Take some minutes to read and memorize a verse during your quiet time: Practice it repeatedly until it sinks in. Commit it to your memory.

Thy word have I hid in mine heart, that I may not sin against thee. (Psalm 119:11 KJV)

The Word of God is more than just the letters and alphabets. The Bible contains a plethora of stories about faithful witnesses of God's children and servants. Many of the New Testament books are letters of cautionary tales written by Apostle Paul to different churches to offer encouragement, caution believers against lukewarmness and to discourage bad habits from festering.

In some of his epistles, Paul addresses issues plaguing the church. By taking time to meditate on them, you can learn a great deal and find applications to your daily challenges.

This can be done anytime of the day, however I strongly recommend doing it early in the morning at a set time and place before you leave your home.

Pray always: Prayer is crucial in your walk with God and to stay connected. You can simultaneously perform your daily prayer and devotion or quiet time. It's essential because everyday life can be hard, gruesome and unpredictable. Prayer doesn't change who God is, but it changes us. There are many Scriptures that exhort us to pray.

Pray without ceasing. (I Thessalonians 5:17 NKJV)

Do not be anxious about anything, but in every situation, by prayer and petition, with thanksgiving, present your requests to God. (Philippians 4:6 NIV)

Is anyone among you in trouble? Let them pray. Is anyone happy? Let them sing songs of praise. (James 5:13 NIV)

Be joyful in hope, patient in affliction, faithful in prayer. (Romans 12:12 NIV)

Prayer was important to Jesus while he was on the earth; for example He prayed all night before picking the 12 apostles. And as Christians we are supposed to emulate Jesus, so we must prioritize prayer as part of our lifestyle. Prayer is our lifeline and connection to God, giving us access to Him. Prayer makes us more like Jesus and shows us the heart of God.

There were days in my life I would wake up crestfallen, crushed, defeated and abandoned. My wife and kids being far away from me and the experience of loneliness here in Canada. To top it off, my life was busy with dozens of tasks to do each day with no support.

Who likes going through these kinds of storms? No one and neither do I. However, I know that my Redeemer lives. I also know that there's always a reason for everything God does and permits. The circumstances I was in could either keep me away from God or draw me near to Him. It was my choice and I chose Him and I chose to hold on in the place of prayer.

Prayer is highly effective for warring against the schemes of the Devil.

For our struggle is not against flesh and blood, but against the rulers, against the authorities, against the power of this dark world and against the spiritual forces of evil in the heavenly realms. (Ephesians 6:12 NIV)

Prayers provides us with an effective tool to win the constant battles that we are in. It is only through prayer that we can gain strength and faith to run the race to the finish line victoriously.

Write it down: When you spend time in devotion or meditation, use either a hard copy journal or the notes on your cellphone to write down salient points and revelation. Writing them down is one sure way to commit things to memory. This is a way of exercising the brain with neurological benefits that help preserve it by keeping it sensitive. Thoughts, emotions and feelings are at work during devotional study. When you are meditating, you introspect and reflect. You can closely observe yourself. These notes need to be dated to serve as a reference in the future. They can also help you to review where and how you might need help. The act of writing is an honest exercise and can build a strong foundation for a Christian to overcome sinful tendencies.

The art of writing is phenomenal and God encourages us to write down our revelations and make it visible.

Then the Lord replied: "Write down the revelation and make it plain on tablets so that a herald may run with it. For the revelation awaits an appointed time; it speaks of the end and will not prove false. Though it lingers, wait for it; it will certainly come and will not delay." (Habakkuk 2:2 NIV)

Write therefore the things that you have seen, those that are and those that are to take place after this. (Revelation 1:19 ESV)

When you write something down, you are bringing it to life so you don't forget because the faintest pen is stronger than strongest memory.

For the word of God is living and active, sharper than any two-edged sword, piecing to the division of soul and of spirit, of joints and of marrow, and discerning the thoughts and intentions of the heart. (Hebrews 4:12 ESV)

Conversations between you and God need to be written and documented. The whispers, the small still voice and the inner convictions can all form part of the larger vision. This way, you will not forget.

Remember, then, what you received and heard. Keep it, and repent. If you will not wake up, I will come like a thief, and you will not know at what hour I will come against you. (Revelation 3:3 ESV)

God told the prophet Isaiah to write.

Then the Lord said to me, "Take a large scroll and write on it with an ordinary pen: Maher-Shalal-Hash-Baz." (Isaiah 8:1 NIV)

Writing what God says speaks volumes and connotes your commitment and devotion. It also helps you fight memory retention problems. Holding the pen in between your fingers and seeing the coarse scratches it makes on paper can help you rediscover yourself at special moments.

Get involved in your local church: When it is impossible to attend a church service in person, then join the service online. Become a worker in your local church, belong to a group or department and always find something to do in the house of God. It is rewarding.

And he gave the apostles, the prophets, the evangelists, the shepherds, and teachers, to equip the saints for the work of ministry, for building up the body of Christ. (Ephesians 4:11-12 ESV)

So then, as we have opportunities, let us do good to everyone, and especially to those who are of the household of faith. (Galatians 6:10 ESV)

After the service, don't just pick up your belongings and leave unless you have commitments. There is so much work to be done in the house of God. Avoid the temptation to become complacent and casual. Despite our hectic schedules, we should not fall for the subtle temptation of thinking we are doing all there is to do in the house of God.

Once you discover who you are in Christ Jesus and understand what skills and spiritual gifts you possess, you will be able to identify which department of the church that you're a great fit for. You can start doing things like cleaning, dusting the chairs, mopping, picking up trash and plenty of other things to maintain the church environment. Or you could set up the stage and instruments. Though you may think these tasks are little, God sees it all through a different prism.

We live in a fast-paced environment where people find socializing challenging. Be that as it may, we must find time to create the right balance and be hospitable to fellow church members. You will find it exhilarating and spiritually uplifting when a fellow brother or sister comes over for a great home-cooked meal amid a warm conversation. It can be life changing and heart warming for a newcomer to your church.

Every activity in your church presents an opportunity to serve and contribute to kingdom advancement. Build relationships with serious believers that edify the body of Christ and offer opportunities to serve one another.

Church is not only meant to be on a Sunday. Endeavour to join the midweek service, prayer meetings, small groups and Bible studies. This will help you interact with other believers to get sound and expository teaching of the Bible. This affords you opportunities to ask questions. You can also follow an online Bible study. Ask the Holy Spirit to help you identify the right one and your pastor can also make recommendations.

Fast: A fast is a spiritual exercise which the Scripture admonishes us to engage in. Humans are designed to feast on God as described by the psalmist:

O God, you are my God; earnestly I seek you; and my soul thirsts for you; my flesh faints for you, as in a dry and weary land where there is no water...my soul will be satisfied as with fat and rich food. (Psalm 63:1-5 ESV).

There is spiritual delight to be found in Christ that far exceeds the physical diet and fasting is one such way.

Blessed are those who hunger and thirst for righteousness, for they shall be satisfied. (Matthew 5:6 ESV)

More than your stomach wants food, your soul should desire to know God. God probes the edges of our deep spiritual hunger and thirst. Often, the weakness of our hunger for God is not because He is unsavoury, but because we keep ourselves preoccupied with carnal things.

"Fasting if conceive of it truly, must not be confined to the question of food and drink; fasting should really be made to include abstinence from anything which is legitimate in and of itself for the sake of some special spiritual purpose. There are many bodily functions which are right and normal and perfectly legitimate, but which for special peculiar reasons in certain circumstances should be controlled and abstain from. That is fasting." -Martyn Lloyd-Jones

The point here is that fasting is not only about abstaining from bodily food and drink. The issue is controlling and abstaining from everything that can substitute for God or anything that can stand in the way of being true disciple.

So, you cannot become my disciple without giving up everything you own. (Luke 14:33 NLT)

Oxen, fields and marriage can keep you out of the kingdom of God if not controlled.

Fasting is one of the few activities that has proven to be beneficial to man both physically and spiritually. It helps focus your mind and body for a spiritual cause. It is strongly recommended you engage in a fast from time to time as the Spirit leads.

Sing to Him: Cultivate the habit of singing praises to God. In the last few years of my life, it is becoming nearly impossible to jumpstart any personal prayer session without singing several praises or worship songs first.

Let everything that has breath praise the Lord. (Psalm 150:6 NIV)

What is it about praising or worshipping God through songs, psalms, hymns that is so important?

Singing is not an option in the Bible; it is a command.

Let the word of Christ dwell in you richly, teaching and admonishing one another in all wisdom, singing psalms and hymns and spiritual songs, with thankfulness in your hearts to God. (Colossians 3:16 ESV)

And do not get drunk with wine, for that is debauchery, but be filled with the Spirit, addressing one another in psalms and hymns and spiritual songs, singing and making melody to the Lord with your heart. (Ephesians 5:18-19 ESV)

Praise is God's food and we have been commanded to sing praises to God. When you sing, you're obeying God's command and deepening roots in His word. When you sing, you're glorifying God.

When you worship and sing about the Lord's goodness, you are helping unbelievers and evangelizing in a way.

Sing to him, sing praises to him; tell of all his wondrous works! (Psalm 105:2 ESV)

"Good corporate worship will naturally be evangelistic." -Tim Keller

When you sing, you are spiritually strengthened for victory after all kinds of trials. There is joy that comes with singing. Even in suffering, sing.

The Bible says:

Is anyone cheerful? Let him sing praise. (James 5:13b ESV)

For you have been my help, and in the shadow of your wings I will sing for joy." (Psalm 63:7 ESV)

Singing often produces joy and joy often produces singing and when you study Scripture you will see how they're intricately tied.

Hear No Evil, See No Evil and Speak No Evil: I know the "hear no evil and see no evil" part is giggly as there are things you simply just can't control. But you must be deliberate about it.

Download a gospel music app in your cellphone. In your car, try to not play music that doesn't glorify the Lord . God wants us to listen to things that honour Him. Avoid filthy and vulgar languages. Steer clear of locker room talk that doesn't edify the body of Christ.

Scripture tells us;

Finally, brothers and sisters, whatever is true, whatever is noble, whatever is right, whatever is pure, whatever is lovely, whatever is admirable – if anything is excellent or praiseworthy – think about such things. (Philippians 4:8 NIV)

But immorality or any impurity or greed must not even be named among you, as is proper among saints; and there must be no filthiness and silly talk, or coarse jesting, which are not fitting, but rather giving of thanks. Ephesians 5:3-4 NASB)

God wants us to listen to holy things just as we have been warned to desist from seeing the nakedness of others (Genesis 9:20-24). Stop watching adult movies, magazines and pornography.

Behold, I am coming like a thief. Blessed is the one who stays awake and keeps his clothes, so that he will not walk about naked, and men will not see his shame. (Revelation 16:15 NASB)

So, the king of Assyria will lead away stripped and barefoot the Egyptian captives and Cushite exiles, young and old, with buttocks bared – to Egypt's shame. (Isaiah 20:4 NIV)

Those who display their naked bodies and cleavages are committing shameful acts.

Clearly, the Scripture warns believers to not listen or watch things that involve sinful behaviours. Do not listen, speak, or watch anything that will desensitize you to sin and corrupt your morals.

Enjoy the fellowship of believers: When we come together in fellowship, we teach and learn from each other. They early Christians clearly emphasized the importance of fellowship.

They devoted themselves to the apostle's teaching and to the fellowship, to the breaking of bread and to prayer. Everyone was filled with awe at the many wonders and signs performed by the apostles. All the believers were together and had everything in common. (Acts 2:42-22 NIV)

The Bible also says,

As iron sharpens iron, so one person sharpens another. (Proverbs 27:17 NIV)

Fellowship is a mutual bond that believers have with Christ Jesus that puts us in deep, eternal relationship with one another. The word, 'fellowship' comes from Greek word koinonia, which means partnership or participation and it basically describes the situation of individuals who are working together in spiritual matters. The Bible encourages us to come together in fellowship.

And let us not neglect our meeting together, as some people do, but encourage one another, especially now that the day of his return is drawing near. (Hebrews 10:25 NLT)

It means that isolation or 'go it alone' should be discouraged. Fellowship sharpens a man and cheers the spirits. Apostle Paul says,

God is faithful, who has called you into the fellowship of his Son, Jesus Christ our Lord. (1 Corinthians 1:9 NIV)

Many Christians believe that we can have fellowship with one another simply based on our belief in Christ. But John said this type of fellowship is for believers who are cleansed by the blood of Jesus.

But if we walk in the light, as he is in the light, we have fellowship with one another, and the blood of Jesus, his Son, purifies us from all sin. (1 John 1:7 NIV)

And now why do you wait? Rise and be baptized and wash away your sins, calling on his name. (Acts 22:16 ESV)

Thus, it is not just for believers, but for baptised believers because our sins are washed away in baptism. There are both spiritual and physical benefits in fellowshipping together with believers.

Let us think of ways to motivate one another to acts of love and good works. And let us not neglect our meeting together as some

people do, but encourage one another, especially now that the day of his return is drawing near. (Hebrews 10:24-25 NLT)

Wise and profitable conversation sharpens a believer's wits and add to his store of knowledge. Fellowship puts a briskness in the life of a Christian and makes such a Christian to be at peace with themselves in their souls. By this practice, we grow in discipline toward God's work, and we hold each other accountable in our walk with God. It helps us grow our prayer lives and prepare us in the journey ahead. We must desire to come alongside each other to counsel one another, and build up one another. Fellowship gives us a mental picture of who God is and makes us stronger in faith. Fellowship reminds us that we are not alone and helps us to grow by receiving godly counsel from one another and those who have oversight function over us.

Seek godly counsel: You must pursue godly counsel.

Listen to advice and accept instructions, that you may gain wisdom in the future. Many are the plans in the mind of a man, but it is the purpose of the Lord that will stand. (Proverbs 19:20-21 ESV)

One sure way of making the right decisions in God's will is to seek godly counsel especially as a teenager, youth or single adult. Major decisions in the choice of who to marry, course of study, career path to follow or a vocation all require that a person should seek Godly counsel.

A very popular example in the Bible about a man who listened and followed an unwise counsel was Rehoboam, Solomon's son as contained in 1 King 12:1-16.

Soon after Rehoboam was enthroned as a king, he was confronted by his subjects who beseeched him to treat them compassionately. Right off the bat, King Rehoboam consulted the same old men who had counseled his father, Solomon before making his decision. The old men wisely advised him to treat the people with compassion as they had demanded. Sadly, Rehoboam did not heed that advice and he went further to consult his peers, who gave him bad and unwise counsel. His peers told him to ignore his subjects and treat them as he had wished. Rehoboam had two counsels and it was up to him as the king to choose which of the counsels he was going to follow. Unfortunately, Rehoboam followed the unwise counsel and lost most of his kingdom.

The point is not to claim that young people always give unwise counsel or that wise counsel is exclusive right of the older people, No. It doesn't always follow.

The Scripture encourages us to seek counsel from wise people.

Walk with the wise and become wise, for a companion of fools suffers harm. (Proverbs 13:20 NIV)

It depends on who you are taking counsel from. Is the fellow walking in the Spirit? An old person who doesn't walk in the Spirit will spew out gibberish as counsel regardless of their age. On the other hand, a younger fellow who walks in the Spirit and lives by the Word of God will offer wise and godly counsel.

There is a way that seems right to a man, but its end is the way of death. (Proverbs 14:12 KJV)

All of us listen to other people in our lives at some point or the other but we often run into trouble whenever we listen to the wrong counsels. If you search from a sincere heart, you find people who will tell you what God says in His word per time concerning any issues. Your pastor is one such person.

Stay away from anything that is toxic and anathema to the word of God. Severe ties with friends or end relationships that tend to impede your walk with God, or which interferes with the working of the Holy Spirit in you.

Don't be too big to take corrections. Regardless of your parents' age, financial status, and health condition, listen to their advice. Listen to your elders and spiritual parents as well. Pay attention to whatever they are pointing at and honour them so that you may live long. They may not always be right but don't shut them down or treat them in disdain.

When you must correct anyone, do it with wisdom and ask for the help of the Holy Spirit. As much as you can, avoid correcting someone publicly especially adults and always keep the intention pure, honest, and objective. Correction should be driven by love. When Jesus corrected people, He did so in love. In some circumstances – such as when He was confronted with the hypocrisy of the Pharisees (Matthew 23) – He rebuked them harshly, yet out of love and for their benefits even though they responded poorly to His rebuke. Unlike Martha, a gentle correction was all that was required (Luke 10:38-42) and the Bible tells us that Martha remained one of Jesus' dearest friends (John 11:5).

Correction or discipline can sometime be uncomfortable and only few people like it. Oftentimes, because of our pride, it's hard to receive correction graciously. The Scripture says in Proverbs that heeding correction is a sign of wisdom and understanding (Proverbs 15:31-32). Godly correction helps us to examine our ways, reroute our direction and follow Jesus more closely.

Christianity is a way of life because we see its application in our everyday life. Let me start this point by emphasizing that if Christianity is nothing more to you than eternal life insurance policy and has no impact on how you live and relate with others, then you are missing the point of salvation.

We need the everyday discipline of staying focused and keeping our eyes on the big picture. Hold tight that which you have received and don't abandon the ancient landmark.

We must pay the most careful attention, therefore, to what we have heard, so we do not drift away. (Hebrews 2:1 NIV)

Nothing puts me off like the inconsistencies of fellow Christians. In fact, nothing seems to turn unbelievers away from Christianity more than that of inconsistency, seeing believers say one thing yet do another thing. Painfully and unfortunately, this is prevalent among Christians today, impeding our witness especially in the era where our lives have become the mirror which the world looks to as gospel.

It is quite simple to just be mediocre Christians and when the chips are down and the going gets tough, we fall apart and crash like giant dominos. This is partly because we are flabby, flimsy, and shapeless on the inside. We easily trip because we are carrying that extra baggage in our lives that are not helping us to travel light. When we journey heavy, holding and clutching onto extra things, we stumble easily and get entangled with encumbrances. Therefore, we often get distracted by whatever the world presents to us as important. It's by walking in the Spirit that we can please God. This is the numero uno.

Prayer points

1. Father, the Holy Spirit is the most important thing that I need to be able to successfully work with You daily. Fill me with Your Holy Spirit in the mighty name of Jesus.
2. Father, take away every proud spirit in me and replace it with the spirit of humility so that I can heed to godly counsel in the mighty name of Jesus.
3. Dear Lord, by Your mercy, open my spiritual eyes that I will see areas of my life where I need to take correction and help me to reroute my way back to you in the mighty name of Jesus.

CONCLUSION

_____

THE ULTIMATE END

Let us hear the conclusion of the whole matter: Fear God and keep his commandments: for this is the whole duty of man. (Ecclesiastes 12:13 KJV)

Events stir us and draw a crowd, but it is only the truth that changes a life. Jesus wants to change our lives forever.

There's a drama in great music that conveys powerful message. My daughter, Emmanuella recently has been learning how to skillfully play piano and violin as part of her vocation. Whenever she plays, I observe and listen to the sounds with keen interest. In general, whenever a skillful pianist or violinist plays an instrument, moments of pauses and modulations in volume are observed. Some sections of the music are dulcet, some soft while others are reflective and still others are places where the sound crescendos in victory and excitement. In great movies the plot twists and turns until it reaches a climax of the storyline, and this is the time when the viewer is in cliff-hanger and cannot wait to watch the movie to the end. They must get to the end even if it means staying awake all night to find out what exactly happened to the characters in the movie.

The Scripture is even more dramatic than the music or movie analogy. The Bible is more than a compendium and it's replete with great stories for our lifelong learnings. The Bible catalogues some of these earth-shaking stories:

At His pleasure, the Red Sea divided, and its waters stood up.

At His bidding, the earth opened, and the Jewish rebels were swallowed up.

He made the flood to cover the earth

When he ordered it, the sun stood still and even went back.

He made the Ravens feed the prophet.

He empowered a young boy to take a stand against a giant

He caused an iron axe-head to float on water, defying the principles of floatation.

He even tamed the lions and became the fourth person in the fiery furnace.

He caused a fish to swallow a reluctant prophet who was running away from Him.

He turned water into wine at the wedding in Cana.

He raised Lazarus from the death after four days

The list can go on and on….

The birth and death of our savior Jesus Christ was similarly dramatic (Luke 2:1-20 & Luke 15:21-38) let alone the miracles that Jesus himself performed. Starting with the miracle of turning of water into wine at the wedding in Cana, raising Lazarus from dead, the various healings he wrought and finally, the miraculous resurrection.

Here are a few suggestions to fully appreciate what Jesus had done. Everyday, we are often swallowed up in the flurry of activities, but amid this busyness try find some time to be quiet. Find the right balance. Personal devotion for self-reflection and introspection is important. Find time to sit alone with God and allow the holiness of His greatness to overwhelm you for a moment. Reflect of what happened in the garden of Eden and remind yourself that His death on the cross reveals that:

Jesus Christ is not like any other 'god'

His love for mankind was the agape type

His sacrifice on the cross was accepted on our behalf by God the Father

This life is not all there is

Allow these truths to lead you into tears, sober reflection and finally, into worship. Let it sink in and let it overwhelm you deeply. Respond to Jesus's offer of forgiveness, reconciliation, and a new life. The stories in the bible are not mere dramas or Shakespearean words or some sort of cunningly divine fables, those are profound gospel truths. If indeed, Jesus died for you and rose again, then He's worth following with every ounce of strength that you have got. He's worth serving with every drop of your blood. Digest these truths and take them personally.

Conduct a soul searching right now, if Jesus should come now where will you spend your eternity? Jesus did for us what we could not do for ourselves, that is to reconcile us with our creator. Jesus is inviting you to surrender, he is calling you to come home, and he is reaching out to you, and you don't have to retreat. His death was the greatest sacrifice the world has ever known, and his resurrection was an affirmation that the payment was satisfactory and acceptable. If we embrace the reality of these truths, it will change our lives. Let these truths sink in to avoid the second death.

From Jesus' conversation with Nicodemus in John 3, here's what comes to my mind about the changes that take place in the life cycle of a typical butterfly:

A crawling caterpillar is born from an egg and immediately begins to destroy vegetation. The caterpillar then enters a kind of "death" in a self-made coffin called a chrysalis where he seemingly lies lifeless for weeks. Then through the process of metamorphosis this "dead" caterpillar is transformed and "born again" as it emerges from his tomb as a gorgeous butterfly. Of course, after a few weeks that butterfly will also die.

If you have been born once, you will die twice, but if you are born twice, you will die only once.

It may sound awful, but the gospel is so profound, and its good news is that Jesus Christ died and resurrected to restore our life spiritually. Jesus is the word of life and if we are obedient enough through faith, we would be resurrected from the dead to live eternal.

For we died and were buried with Christ by baptism. And just as Christ was raised from the dead by the glorious power of the Father, now we also may live new lives. (Romans 6:4 NLT)

"But God is so rich in mercy, and he loved us so much, that even though we were dead because of our sins, he gave us life when he raised Christ from the dead. (It is only by God's grace that you have been saved. (Ephesians 2:4-5 NLT)

Jesus replied, I tell you the truth, unless you are born again, you cannot see the kingdom of God. (John 3:3 NLT)

This is the second birth also called 'born again'. For those who will experience the second birth and remain faithful to the end, the second death has no power (Revelation 20:6). Everyone of us is born at least once and all of us die at least once. Howbeit, if we are not born again in Christ, we will die twice, physically, and then spiritually in hell. But if we are born twice, first physically and second spiritually, we will only die once, and we shall not experience the second death.

Do whatever it takes…

The life here in this part of eternity can be a difficult place to traverse and often gruesome and fleeting. But heaven is a beautiful place because of its splendor and there we find rest. God has given us rest in our home beyond the vale. Heaven is a beautiful place because it has no pain or anguish. Heaven is a beautiful place because nothing sinful is there. What a joy on the day that you will finally behold the glorious face of sweet Jesus. What a joy to be able to share a table and associate with the Bible greats and faithful of all ages!

It will be worth it! We will have the comfort that lasts throughout eternity.

Heaven is a beautiful place that is filled with glory and grace.

Everyone wants to go to heaven but not everyone will go to heaven. Total obedience is required if anyone wants to enter this beautiful and gorgeous place.

Not everyone who calls out to me, 'Lord! Lord!' will enter the kingdom of Heaven. Only those who actually do the will of my father in heaven will enter. (Matthew 7:21 NLT)

Do whatever it takes...

Every morning when you wake up say to yourself,

I will not flinch in the face of adversity or hesitate in the face of hardship. I will not negotiate at the table of the enemy of the gospel of Christ. I won't give in or give up. I won't throw in the towel or carve into the demand of Satan. I won't shut up or remain silence. I won't burn up until I have prayed up and stayed up for the cause of my saviour.

I am a disciple of Jesus Christ, and I must remain vigilant until He shows up or until I drop dead. I've dedicated my whole life to being His disciple here on earth and I am committed to doing whatever it takes.

How much more time have you got to live before death comes or rapture takes place? How long before the opportunities before you end? You don't know. You just don't know. How long that window will stay open, no one else knows. But one thing is certain: it expires. A day is coming, the day of reckoning, the day the Lord will be on His judgement throne, when all accounts shall be reconciled. On that day, you will render accounts of your stewardship before your creator and the only words more painful than "If I had known and had I known …" will be Too late!

INSPIRATION...

I have written this book to help you (myself inclusive) remain watchful and not to let down our guard as you journey through this side of eternity.

Help to Grow - prayer and Scriptural nuggets - for starters was an inspiration that I caught during this global pandemics.

Like I mentioned earlier, I'm not an expert in praying and I do not intend to give such impression.

However, I am acutely and biblically aware of the need for God's glory in the life of the generation that precedes us. So, I'm passionate about young persons encountering Jesus early in life and committed to helping and encouraging children, teenagers and young adults to do the same. I'm committed to helping people to build a real-life faith and have a personal encounter with Jesus through relationship with God in the areas of prayer, personal devotion and quiet time with God.

Printed in the United States
by Baker & Taylor Publisher Services